No. 1227
$15.95

333
EASY-TO-BUILD
FUN PROJECTS
FOR YOUR HOME
BY JEAN C. STONEBACK
AND GENE WEISBECKER

TAB BOOKS Inc.
BLUE RIDGE SUMMIT, PA. 17214

FIRST EDITION

FIRST PRINTING

MAY 1981

Copyright © 1981 by TAB BOOKS Inc.

Printed in the United States of America

Reproduction or publication of the content in any manner, without express permission of the publisher, is prohibited. No liability is assumed with respect to the use of the information herein.

Library of Congress Cataloging in Publication Data

Stoneback, Jean.
   333 easy-to-build fun projects for your home.

   "TAB book #1227."
   Includes index.
   1. Handicraft.   I. Weisbecker, Gene, joint author.   II. Title.
TT157.S77   745.5   80-28404
ISBN 0-8306-9655-5
ISBN 0-8306-1227-O (pbk.)

Contents

    Preface   10

1 Home Decoration Ideas   11
    Hanging Plant Holder 11
    Table Savers for Flower Pots 12
    Outside Hanging Lamp 12
    Stained Glass Swag Lamp 14
    Coconut Shell Lamp 15
    Quart Jar and Wine Bottle Lamps 16
    Swag Light 17
    Bed Lamp 18
    Tin Can Lanterns 19
    Lamp Base 20
    Large Clay Planter 22
    Milk Carton Vase 23
    Hanging Planter From a Milk Carton 24
    Planter Bookends 25
    Lawn or Plant Birds 27
    Floor Plant Stand 27
    Hanging Flowerpot Holder 28
    Flower Arranging Vase 28
    Curtain Pulls 29
    Sand Scenes 30
    Sponge Garden 33
    Driftwood Planter 33
    Mushroom for Decorating Plants 33
    Glitter Wall Decoration 34
    Branches and Berries Picture 36
    Wall Decoration of Chinese Characters 36
    Flower Girl Picture 36
    Leather Picture 38
    Small Pie Pan Pictures 40
    Cake Pan Pictures 41
    Silhouette Picture 41
    Seashell Picture 43

Wooden Rings Picture 43
Pennsylvania Dutch Hex Signs 44
Leopard Doorstop 46
Monk Doorstop 48
Mirror Decoration 49
Large Fruitcake Can Redecorated 49
A Small Screen 50
Stenciled Place Mats 51
Braided Mats 52
Hair Spray Cover-Up 52
Gourd Ashtray 54
Cork Coasters 55
Butterfly Mobile 56
Clay Trivet 56
Cheese Box Ottoman 56
Smoking Stand 59
Curtain Room Divider 60
Salt and Pepper Shakers 62
Wooden Tray 62
Wastepaper Basket Magic 63
Refrigerator Stickups 64
Gourds On a Braid 65
Pot Holders 65
Handle Holder 66
Tray Fun 66
Paper Napkin Holder 67
Birch Bark Napkin Holder 67
Etched Glass 68
String Pot 68
Rattan Basket 70
Tin Can or Tin Can Lid Coasters 72
Yard Sign 74
Cutting Board 76
Wooden Spoon Decor 76
Conch Shell 77
Re-doing An Old Bathroom Sink 77
Old Dough Box 77
Shadow Box 77
Key Hanger 79
Popsicle Trellis for a Plant 81
Door Bells 81
Sit-Upon 81
Shelf Covering 82
Scrubbers 82
Barn Lumber Bookcase 82
Barn Lumber Cookie Cutter Holder 83
Picture Frames 83
Kitchen Table 83
Nail Keg Stools and Lamp Holders 84
Marble Top Table 84
Step Ladder Fun 84

2 Personalized Gifts 85
Clover Leaf Jewelry 85
Brass Wire Pin 85

Wooden Bird or Flower Pin   86
Jewelry From Pull-Off Caps of Metal Cans   86
Wire and Bead Ring   88
Tin Can Bracelet   89
Aztec Sun God Pendant   89
Heart Pin   90
Rubber Cord Bracelet   90
Jewelry Box for Dad   92
Star Earrings   94
Leather Pendant   94
Clay Mouse Pin   95
Grape Pin   95
Slate Pin   96
Lens Pendant   97
Modern Clay Pendant   99
Owl Felt Pin   99
Arrow Head Necklace   99
Old Snowflake Glass   100
Tiepin   100
Feather Stationary   101
Clove Apple   101
Leather and Foil Barrette   102
Glasses Case   103
Comb Case   103
Tiny Cushion Scents   103
Dollhouse   104
Wastebasket   105
Yarn Holder   106
Desk Blotter   108
Butterfly Bobby Pin   109
Flower Basket   109
Foam Ball Pin Cushion   109
Bookworm Bookends   110
Pencil Holder   111
Covered Hangers   112
Cheese Cutting Board   113
Snow Jar   114
Mason Jar Gardens   114
Cocktail Apron   114
Barbecue Apron   115
Stenciled Scarf   116
Corsage Holder   117
Watering Can Fun   117
Embossed Silver Box   118
Letter Opener   119
Hand Print   120
Wooden Hangers   121
Easel Picture   121
Spice Rope   125
Terrariums   126
Straw Wreaths   127
Salad Bowl Gardening   127
Cardboard Dolls   128
Fancy Jelly Covers   128
Pine Needle Art—Pine Needle Shapes   128
Merry-Go-Round Mobile   129

Water Garden   129
Macaroni Beads   130

3 Brighten Up the Holidays   131

Christmas Door Decoration   131
Angel Wall Decoration   132
Bell Pull for Christmas   133
Christmas Window Decoration   136
Candlestick Holders   136
Foam Ball Christmas Decoration   136
Kissing Ring   138
Milkweed Pod Angel   139
Gem Tree   139
Della Robbia Wreath   140
Pine Cone Christmas Tree   141
Swedish Kissing Ball   141
Christmas Bells From Paper Cups   142
Triple Candle Holder   143
Door Handle Cover   143
Christmas Tree Ornament   143
Halloween Mobile   144
Halloween Skeleton   151
Pumpkin Fun   153
Egg Tree   153
Egg Stand   153
Kitchen Witch   154
Plastic Tomato Basket Decoration for a Door   157
Christmas Centerpiece   158
Winter Time Centerpiece   158
Fancy Easter Eggs   158
Broom Corn Swag   159

4 Party Projects   160

Christmas Sleigh   160
Choirboys for Christmas   160
Standing Angel   161
Sugar Plum Tree   163
Plastic Snowman   163
Christmas Nut Cup   164
Place Cards   168
Pinata   168
Valentine Centerpiece   170
Pine Cone Turkey   171
Paper Posy   171
Valentine Candy Cup   172
Egg Heads   173
Easter Centerpiece   176
Easter Candy Cup   177
Halloween Favor   178
Halloween Nut Cup   179
Prune and Marshmallow Favor   180
Walnut Shell Bouquet   180
Corsage Favors   181
Fancy Balloon   181
Thanksgiving Centerpiece   182
Scarecrow   183

Bridal Shower Centerpiece and Place Mats 184
Baby Shower Centerpiece and Favors 184
Youngsters' Birthday Party Centerpiece and Favors 185
Teenagers' Birthday Party Centerpiece and Favors 185

5 Crafts for Personal Enjoyment 187

Brick Doorstop 187
Belt Holder 187
Peach Stone Ducks 188
Old Fashioned Oil Lamp 188
Walnut Shell Sailboat 190
Burr Porcupine 190
Potato Prints 191
Mister Potato Head 191
Lambkin 192
Treasure Box 194
Ice Candles 195
Clothespin Clip 196
Chessmen From Spools 196
Robot Marionette 197
Paper Bag Puppets 199
Paper Bag Halloween Masks 201
Egg Shell Vase 202
Spatter Print Bridge Tally Card 203
Hanging Basket Lettuce Crisper 204
Jar Pretties 204
Martian Paperweights 204
Name Pins 205
Corn Husk Dolls 206
Apple Dolls 207
Yarn Dollies 208
Depression Plant or Crystal Garden 209
Japanese Garden 210
Sweet Potato Garden 210
Underwater Scene Candle Cover 211
Ant House 214
Memory Box 215
Bookplate 217
Bookmarker 218
Patch Fun 218
Leather Belt 219
African Necklace 220
Scuffs 220
Link Belt 222
Smoke Printing 223
Book Cover 224
Hair Clip for a Page Clip 226
Nature Creations On Notepaper 227
Valentine Cards 227
Easy Christmas Cards 230
Rock Collection 232
Sewing Cards 232
Bird Nest Garden 233
Cutout Signs 233
Key Holders 233
Photo Album Cover 234

Clam Shell Garden 236
Suede Cloth Vest 236
Shoe Shine Mitt 236
Carry-All Bag 237
Collection of Seashells 238
Shell Decor 238
Bill Collector 238
Broomstick Skirt 238
Needle Holder 239
Walnut Shell Turtle 239
Sock Dolls 239
Rag Book 240
Moccasin Decorating 240
Felt Change Purse 240
Felt Pencil Case 240
Flowerpot Base 240
Antique China Piece Plant Holder 241
Autograph Dachshund 241
Mole Toy 241

6 Group Fund Raising Projects   242

Bike Backpack 242
Car Bag 242
Marble Bag 244
Fabric Crayon Craft 245
Muffin Tin Caddy 245
Bottle Lady 246
Cup and Saucer Man 246
Gourd Rattle 247
Coffee Can Banks 247
Swirl Jar 249
Button Art 250
Milkweed Pod Picture 251
Stone Bug Paperweight 253
Brook Clay Figures 253
Reminder Board 254
Soda Carrier Tote Box 255
Easy Candlemaking 255
Indian Headband 257
Wooden Bead Folks and Wildlife 258
Clay Flowers 258
Totem Pole 259
Rock Fun 261
Shell Bird 261
Seed Fun 261
Seed Picture 261
Paper Plate Decor 262

7 Items for Wildlife and Pets   263

Tin Can Bird Feeder 263
Chickadee Feeder 263
Bottle Bird Feeder 263
Gourd Birdhouse 264
Wooden Wren House 265
Suet Baskets and Bird Cakes 265

Dog Collar 266
Cat Collar 267
Decorated Dog Dish 267
Dog Blanket 269
Catnip Bag 269
Bird Cage Cover 270
Scratch Post for a Cat 271
Dog or Cat Bed 272
Mouse Repellent for a Bird Cage 273
Doghouse 273

8 Just for Fun Crafts 274
Spool Toys 274
Ice Hockey Puck 274
Broomstick Horse 274
Bean Board Backdrop 275
Stilts 276
Sand Shovel 277
Horse Tail 278
Rhythm Sticks 279
Tree House 279
Pine Cone Toys 280
Play Blocks 281
Butterfly Net 282
Butterfly Case 282
Butterfly Stretcher 283

9 Recipes and Special Techniques 284
Clay Recipe 284
Recipe for Salt Dough Christmas Tree Decorations 284
Recipe for Soft Clay for Modeling 285
Carving Clay 285
Finger Paint Recipe 285
Recipe for Dried Flower Mix 285
Bubble Blowing Recipe 286
Wrapping Presents 286
Scoring Paper or Cardboard 286
How To Divide Circles Into Six and 12 Equal Parts 286
Curling Paper 288
Enlarging a Pattern 288
Tips On Painting 290
Some Tips On Tracing 292
Pointers On Pastes, Glues and Cements 292
Assembling a Swag Light 293

Index 294

Preface

Whether you enjoy arts and crafts as a hobby, a money saving achievement, as group projects or as fund raisers, this book is for you. You do not need sophisticated equipment, a special education or a large investment to make use of these projects. If you can read and follow directions, you can make any or all of them. The instructions are clear, simple and fully illustrated to add to your enjoyment.

Besides adding glamour to your home, decorating for the holidays, making a party sparkle, making gifts for your friends, your pets and wildlife, you'll find your leisure time will be filled with the joy of making and doing things. There is also the possibility that some crafts might help you add to the pleasure of others. You can teach groups how to make some projects so they can raise funds for their organizations. Wherever your pleasure or your interests lie, above all have fun.

Jean C. Stoneback
Gene Weisbecker

Chapter 1
Home
Decoration Ideas

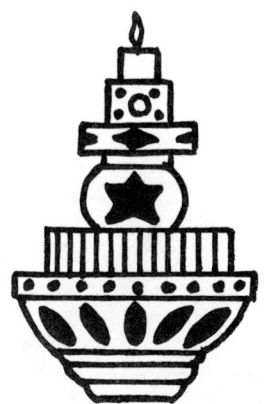

Your home should be a reflection of you. There are many accessories that can reflect your taste and preferences such as lamps, pictures, knickknacks, pillows, astrays and the like.

From all of the ideas in this chapter, you should be able to find many that will suit your taste and add to your decor. Spend some of your leisure time making pretty and useful things to glamorize your home and enjoy the envy of those who see them (Fig. 1-1).

HANGING PLANT HOLDER

Use a large discarded coffee tin for the plant holder.

With a ½" drill bit, drill three holes a little above the middle of the can and equidistant apart. This will be for the cord. Sand smooth and spray the inside and outside of the can with enamel paint.

There are several ways to decorate the can. You can use felt cutouts or designs cut from contact paper. Paint the designs on if you choose.

Glue braid or rickrack around the top of the can. When all decorations are complete, buy yarn about ½" thick that is used for package tying. Cut three pieces, enough to tie a large knot in one end, with some frayed edge and long enough to tie together at the top for hanging.

Insert one end in the hole inside of the can, from the inside out. Tie a large knot and fray the end a little. Do the same with each piece. Tie the other ends to a large ring from a notebook for hanging (Fig. 1-2).

Fig. 1-1. Here are some items that will improve the look of your home.

TABLE SAVERS FOR FLOWER POTS

For these projects you will need large oleo or coffee can lids of plastic. If you wish, you can use permanent marking pens and make a free hand design on the inside of the lid, but remember if you make a mistake it won't come off. You can make a design on paper first by making a circle of the same size as the inside of the lid, or you can trace the design and cut it out. To transfer to plastic, you must use carbon paper and press hard.

When the design is completed on the plastic, use permanent marking pens to color it. This design is outlined to represent stained glass. Place it under flower pots to catch excess water (Fig. 1-3).

OUTSIDE HANGING LAMP

Use self-hardening clay. Roll out on the wrong side of oil cloth with rolling pin until it is about ¼" thick and even. Cut from this a 4" circle and a piece 6½" × 13". While the clay is still wet, make slight lines in the circle rim, ¼" from edge as shown and about 1/16" deep (Fig. 1-4).

Set aside with a damp towel over the clay to keep it from drying out. On a large piece of clay, cut out designs with a sharp tool or compass point. You can use stars, circles, leaf designs or whatever you choose, but do no put them too close together or you will take away the strength you need for the sides of the lamp. Do not let dry.

Fig. 1-2. Hanging planter.

    Mix up a paste of the clay and a little water. Place paste over the marks in the circle base. Pick up the large piece and roll it to fit on top of the base.

    Glue the end together with clay paste. Make sure the closing is smooth and tight. Put aside to dry.

Fig. 1-3. The table saver for plants.

Fig. 1-4. Assemble the outside hanging lamp as shown.

When thoroughly dry, paint inside with white enamel to reflect light. Paint outside with any color desired.

Cut out 1" hole from the center of the circle.

Buy an outside light fixture and swag chain of a desired length in order to hang the lamp. Weave the cord through each link in the chain, leaving enough at one end to go through, with one link on it, and to fasten to the socket.

Leave enough cord beyond the length of chain to reach to a wall socket and fasten the plug. Insert the cord and one chain link through the hole in the top of the lamp. To keep the socket in place, insert a dowel stick through the link that is stuck through the top of the lamp from the inside. Hang the lamp from the hook where the chain ends (Fig. 1-5).

STAINED GLASS SWAG LAMP

A large glass coffee or tea jar that has a deep plastic lid is just the thing for this lamp. Divide the bottle into four even areas around it. To do this, place a strip of paper around the bottle to just meet. Remove the paper, fold in half and then in half again. This will give you four equal parts. Mark the creases with a pencil. Place the paper around the jar again and mark the portions on the jar with a black permanent marking pen. Draw a line from the top to the bottom of the jar.

Mark off each section by making different size areas of different shapes. If you wish, all four sides may be alike or you can make each one different. When all areas are marked, paint each section with glass paints. Use about four or five colors and try not to allow two touching sections to be the same color.

When the glass paint has dried, apply half round leading strips over all the black lines. Use a good cement. Do no overlap the lead; cut at each section.

Drill a ½" hole in the center of the plastic lid and spray paint gold. To complete, follow instructions in the section on general instructions for wiring a swag lamp. Use a tubular bulb (Fig. 1-6).

COCONUT SHELL LAMP

Select a large coconut and saw it in half. Save the juice and scoop out the coconut meat.

Allow the coconut shell to dry thoroughly. Glue three small squares of wood equidistant, measuring about 1½" × 1½" on the base of the bottom coconut shell for legs.

Purchase 1" *dowels* and cut three of them 8" long. Glue them to the rim of the coconut shell. Varnish them with dark stain.

If the rim is too narrow, notch them into the inside of the shell by shaving off the end of the dowel and drilling with holes. Glue small seed pods, acorns and pine cones all around the dowels.

Take the other half of the coconut shell and bore a hole in the top. Add a lamp converter, securing it tightly. Turn it upside down

Fig. 1-5. The completed outside hanging lamp.

Fig. 1-6. Stained glass swag light.

like a hat. Glue it into three dowels that have been drilled, glued and varnished to the bottom half. Plastic wood helps secure tightness.

Decorate the upper half with the same decorations you used on the lower coconut shell. Screw in a light bulb in the socket under the top lid and plug in the cord. You have created an unusual lamp (Fig. 1-7).

QUART JAR AND WINE BOTTLE LAMPS

Select an attractive quart jar or clear wine bottle. Take a soft piece of wood and saw it to fit the top of the jar. Drill a hole in the center of the wooden disc and fit into it a lamp converter that you have purchased in the quarter dollar store.

Put 3" to 4" of sand in the bottom of the jar for weight. Insert articifial flowers into the sand or make a natural scene from a field and forest, using dried weeds, bark, shelf fungus formations, acorns, pine cones or a sea shell from the beach.

Place the disc on the mouth of the jar and glue. Let it dry for a day. Add the lamp converter in the hole. Add a bulb and a small burlap shade.

For the wine bottle lamp, just insert the lamp converter in the mouth of the bottle you have decorated for the base. Add a bulb and shade to the top (Fig. 1-8).

SWAG LIGHT

Make two heavy cardboard circles, one 1-6" in diameter, the other 12" in diameter and 2" wide. From lampshade paper, make a tube 5" in diameter by 12" long.

Put a ½" hole in the center of the small circle and paint both circles a flat black. Glue the tube to the center of the circle.

Enlarge the pattern of sides and make four of heavy cardboard. The open slits in the sides should be as wide as the cardboard circles are thick, with a little extra room so they will slip over the

Fig. 1-7. Coconut shell lamp.

Fig. 1-8. Wine bottle lamp.

circles. Whatever color you make your lampshade tube, paint the sides a color that will go with it.

Buy swag light fixtures at a store and assemble as in Fig. 1-4. Weave the cord in and out of the chain until the chain is as long as you wish the lamp to hang. Hang it on a hook.

While it is hanging, glue the four sides to the circles. Tack wire along the ceiling and down to an outlet (Figs. 1-9 and 1-10).

BED LAMP

Buy four strips of outside corner molding about 1″ by 12″ long. Use lampshade paper 9″ × 33″. Fold the paper so each side is 8″ × 9″ with a 1″ overlap.

Use a board 8″ square and about 1″ thick for the base. Attach a socket for the lamp to the middle of the base, allowing the cord to hang out the back.

Glue paper to the inside corners of the molding, 3″ up from the bottom and overlapping at the back. When set, glue the base to the

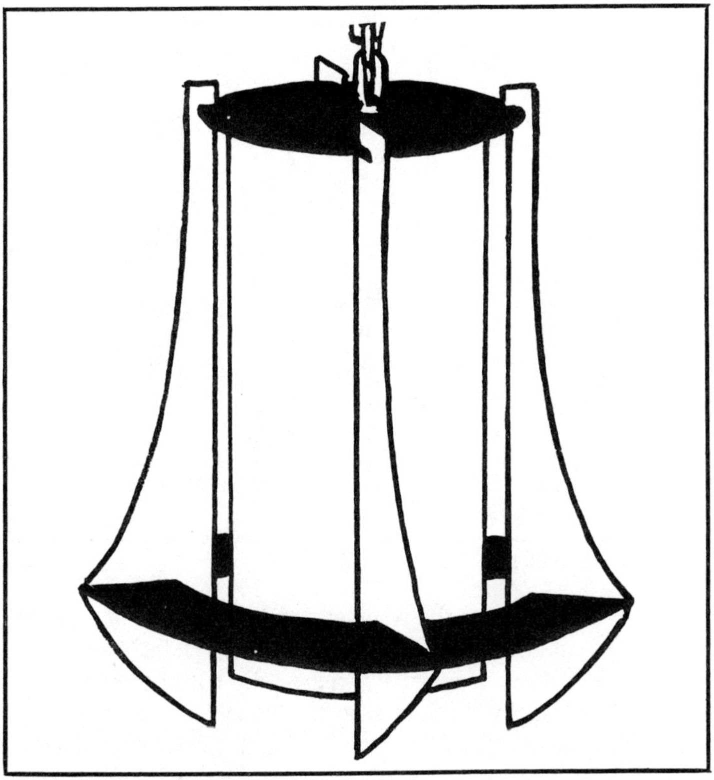

Fig. 1-9. Modern swag light.

inside corners 3" up. You will not need any top for the lamp (Fig. 1-11).

TIN CAN LANTERNS

Use cans that do not have ridges around them and of whatever size you want your lantern to be. Cut off the top and bottom and smooth cut edges.

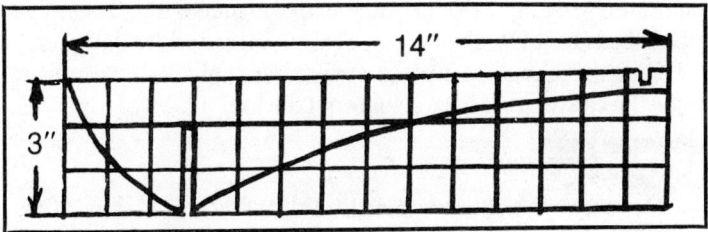

Fig. 1-10. Pattern for the sides for the swag light.

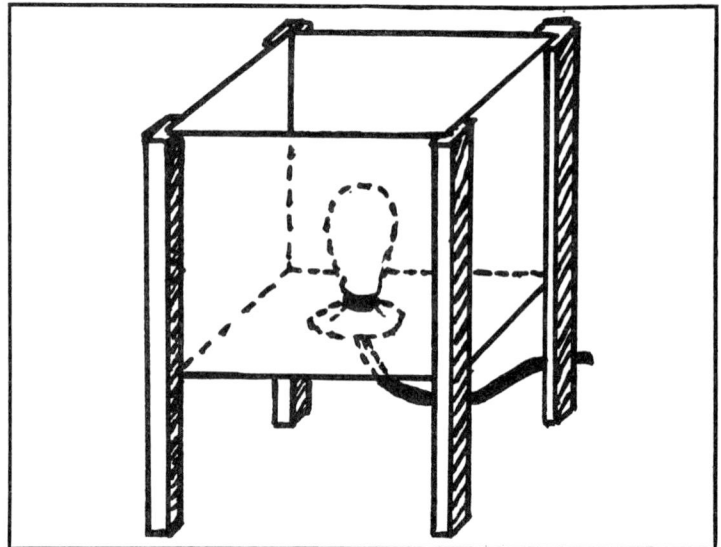

Fig. 1-11. The bed lamp.

Take an extra can, the same size that you are using for the lantern, and cut off only the top. Grease this can on the inside. Fill the can with plaster of paris. When dry, slip out of the can.

Buy funnels, one extra, of a size that will fit over the top of the can with a little overhang as shown in Fig. 1-12. With tin shears, cut off half the length of the small end. Use the extra funnel to make a plaster core as you did with the can. However, you will need to cover the large end of the funnel with cardboard glued on so that the plaster will not run out.

Slip your plaster tin can core into the can you intend to use for your lantern, before you try to punch the holes for the design to keep your can from getting out of shape.

Trace or mark your design off on both sides of the can with marking pens. Notice all dots are not the same size. With the core of plaster in place, use an *ice pick* or drill to make the holes that comprise the design. Do the same with the funnel top. These can be polished and left a silver color or spray painted with a flat black.

Glue the funnel top in place. An ordinary light bulb can be used inside the can with the wire coming out the top.

LAMP BASE

Use a fairly soft plaster and fill a half gallon milk carton. Allow the plaster to thoroughly dry and remove the carton. You can copy the design in Fig. 1-13 or make up your own; you will find straight lines are easier to carve than curves.

Outline the design part that you wish to carve out with a sharp knife about ½" deep. With a chisel, carve out the shaded area. You will need to use sandpaper and emery paper to smooth out the background you have carved.

Do this on all four sides. When carving and smoothing is completed, drill a ½" hole in the middle of the top down to about 1" from the bottom.

On one side drill a ½" hole 1" up from the bottom and to the middle to touch the hole coming down. Clean out with a stiff paint brush.

From the top, insert a brass pipe to about halfway down. This will hold the wire from your lamp. Leave as much above the top as you need to attach your lampshade holder and the part that holds the bulb.

Fig. 1-12. Tin can and funnel lantern.

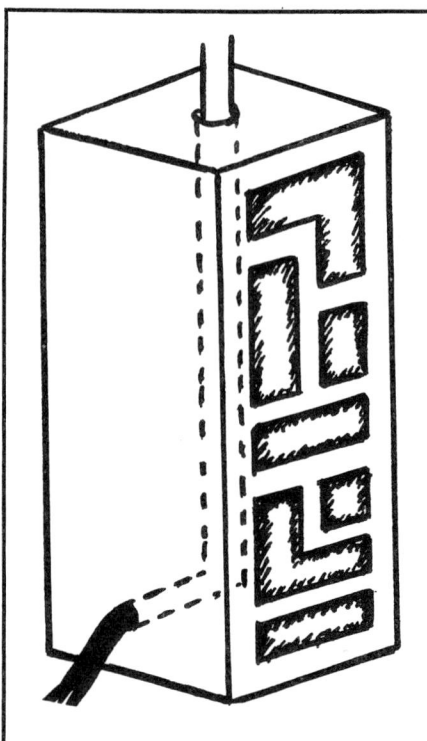

Fig. 1-13. Plaster lamp base.

Push the wire through the pipe and out the side. It will need to be long enough to reach from the lamp to a wall socket and to attach to the bulb at the top. Add a lampshade and your lamp is finished.

LARGE CLAY PLANTER

Look around in secondhand stores and find a china soup bowl that is about 12" in diameter and 2" high. It doesn't have to be that size exactly, but it will make a nice large planter base. Grease the outside of the bowl, and lay it on paper aside from where you are going to work.

Take an old piece of oil cloth 1 yard square. Place it on newspapers on your working area with the wrong side up.

Use self-hardening clay or, if you are into ceramics, the real clay. Roll it out with a rolling pin until you get a circle slightly larger than 12" in diameter, and ¼" thick. Pick it up from the oil cloth and lay it over the greased bottom of the bowl. Use your hands to mold it into the shape of the bowl. Cut off any clay that extends over the edge.

You will have to keep your eye on the clay as it hardens because it will shrink. As it dries, push the clay shape up from the bottom of the bowl a little or it will crack.

Set it aside to become what we refer to as "leather hard"—not dry, but stiff enough to remove from the bowl without losing its shape. You do not want this to dry thoroughly at this time, so it is a good idea to cover it with a damp rag until the other part of your planter is made.

Again, roll out some clay the same thickness, but you will want a strip long enough to go on the top of the bowl and 2" deep. You can find the length you need by cutting a strip of paper and measuring around the top of the bowl. Cut out and remove from the oil cloth.

Remove the rag from the clay bowl and place it on the oil cloth right side up. All around the top rim, make lines about ⅛" deep and ¼" apart. Do the same with one long edge of your long strip and both short ends.

Mix some clay with water to the consistency of paste. Apply generously with your fingers to the top rim of the bowl and the long edge of the strip and ends, when the strip is almost as dry as the bowl. Lift off the strip and curl around the top of the bowl rim, smoothing clay as you go so the seam will not show. Fasten ends together the same way. If both bowl clay and side clay are not of the same hardness at the time of joining, the drier one will shrink and you will have a split.

Using the rounded end of an emery board, scrape out areas on the straight part straight up and down, on an angle or in a design shape all around. When thoroughly dry, paint the bowl with a flat paint or enamel as you desire, but leave scraped out areas the color of the clay. You can fill with good soil and plant with several kinds of greeens. They should all need the same amount of watering and care or some may get over-watered or dried out (Figs. 1-14 and 1-15).

MILK CARTON VASE

You will need to cut off the top of the milk carton only for this project—to a height of 9". Cover the outside of the carton with a light colored contact paper. Allow enough paper to turn inside of the top edge about 1" and under the bottom edge ½". Cut a square from the same paper the size of the bottom of the carton and adhere over the night.

Fig. 1-14. Clay planter.

Buy 30" of outside corner molding ½" wide. Cut two pieces 9" long and two pieces 6" long. Stain your molding a dark color like walnut before adding to the vase.

Glue one long piece to one side of the carton and a short piece to the other side as in Fig. 1-16. The vase can be left plain or decorated with cutouts of leaf designs.

HANGING PLANTER FROM A MILK CARTON

Cut the top off a gallon milk carton. Trace a pattern of the bottom onto a piece of carboard the same thickness as the milk carton, and add ½" all around three sides. Cut out corners. Place inside the open end and glue to hold.

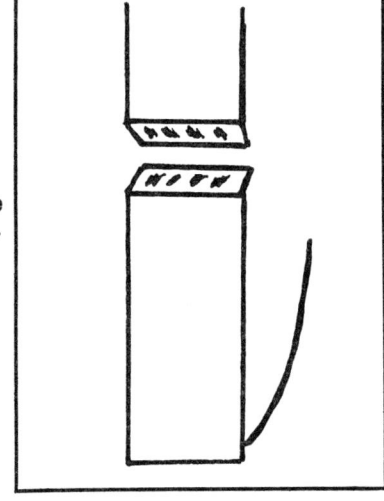

Fig. 1-15. Cutaway view of the planter showing the adhering of clay.

Cover the inside with silver foil, using rubber cement. Cover the outside with gift wrap paper or contact paper, allowing it to overlap to the inside about 1".

Punch ½" holes, two at each end about ½" in from the sides and about 1" from the top. Thread heavy packaging yarn from the outside in, leaving a knot on the outside. Tie all four yarn pieces together for hanging (Fig. 1-17).

PLANTER BOOKENDS

Make a box of heavy cardboard 6" by 6" and 6" high. Seal the sides and bottom well. Grease the inside of the box. Mix up plaster and pour it into the box to a depth of a little more than ½".

Before the plaster hardens, insert 1" dowel sticks that are 3/16" in width, to a depth of about ¼". Insert three on each side and as close to the edge of the box as ¼". Allow plaster to dry thoroughly.

Make another box of heavy cardboard 5" by 5" and deep enough to reach from the plaster in the first box to the top of the first box. Grease the outside of this box.

When plaster in the larger box is completely set, grease the bottom of the smaller box and place it inside the larger one. Now pour plaster into the trough around the edge to the top of the box.

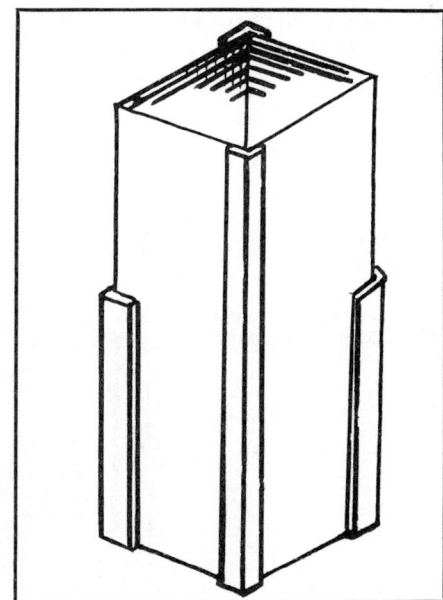

Fig. 1-16. Milk carton vase.

Fig. 1-17. Milk carton planter.

Before this plaster is dry, insert the same size dowel sticks (three again) into one side to a depth of about ½". While the plaster is setting, make another box of the same cardboard the width of the side but only the thickness of the plaster. When the rest of the plaster has set, seal this box to the top of one side, the side with the dowel sticks in it. Seal where it meets the box and grease inside.

Pour plaster into this until it reaches the top. When this plaster has thoroughly set, remove the cardboard. Figure 1-18 shows the construction and insertion of the dowels.

If after removing the cardboard there are lines that show at the seams, or some of the cardboard fuzz is adhering to the plaster, smooth with a very fine emery paper. Fill the box with a little

Fig. 1-18. Assembly detail for the plaster planter bookends.

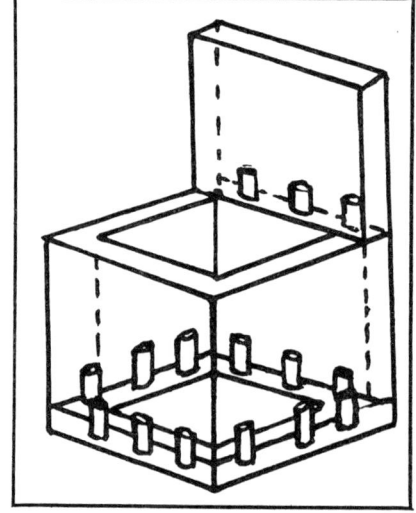

26

gravel for drainage, good soil and plants that require the same type of care (Fig. 1-19).

LAWN OR PLANT BIRDS

If you want to use these birds on the lawn, you will want them bigger than for plants. Enlarge the pattern accordingly. Draw the design on with a soft pencil. Color these birds with a bright colored enamel or use flat paints and spray with *acrylic*.

For the lawn you should use hardboard 1" thick, with a hole drilled in the bottom to take a ⅜" dowel. If the birds are for your indoor plants, use ½" hardboard and ¼" dowel stick (Figs. 1-20 and 1-21).

FLOOR PLANT STAND

This plant stand does double duty because of the two shelves. You will need 14 1" square wooden sticks 30" long for the uprights, and two pieces 12" × 12" × 1" thick for the shelves.

Nail and glue four of the sticks to three sides of one of the squares 3" down from the top. Nail the other sticks 3" from the bottom on to the bottom square on the same sides. Stain your plant stand or color it if you wish, but go over the shelves with a waterproof varnish in case of spills (Fig. 1-22).

Fig. 1-19. The finished planter.

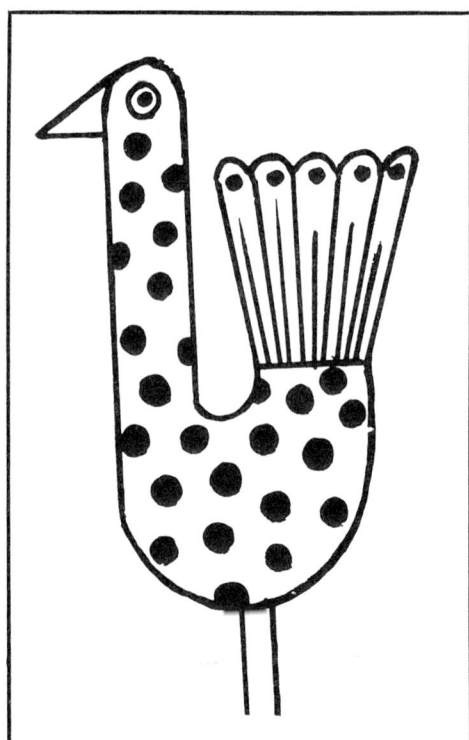

Fig. 1-20. A finished bird.

HANGING FLOWERPOT HOLDER

Enlarge the pattern and trace onto heavy leather (Fig. 1-23). Slit on all heavy lines and punch holes in each of the four corners. Put a heavy cord through the holes with a large knot on the underside. You will want cords at least a foot long. Tie them together at the top.

Dampen the leather with a sponge on both sides. Place a heavy object in the center and hang the holder up. It will stretch into the shape shown in Fig. 1-24. When this shape is reached, remove the heavy object and let the leather dry. It will hold a small pot.

FLOWER ARRANGING VASE

Start with a small or large plastic oleo container. If you wish to change the color, spray paint. When dry, fill ¼ full of sand or plaster of paris for weight.

Punch ¼" holes about ¼" apart in top. These will hold the stems in place and help you make a good arrangement (Fig. 1-25).

CURTAIN PULLS

Cut a large empty spool from thread in half. Glue a large bead in the hole at the flare end and a large bead at the other end. Make sure the holes of the beads are at the ends for the threading cord. Paint the spool a bright color enamel. Thread the cord, leaving a large knot at the bottom.

Paint a large spool of the color desired. Insert upholsterer's tacks around the center. Glue a braid around each end. Glue a large bead at the bottom. From the top, glue a large bead, then a smaller one and still a smaller one. Thread and knot as before.

Cut the large spool in half. Drill holes about ¼" apart around the spool. Insert tees in each hole. Paint the entire spool and tees

Fig. 1-21. Hardboard is required to make the bird.

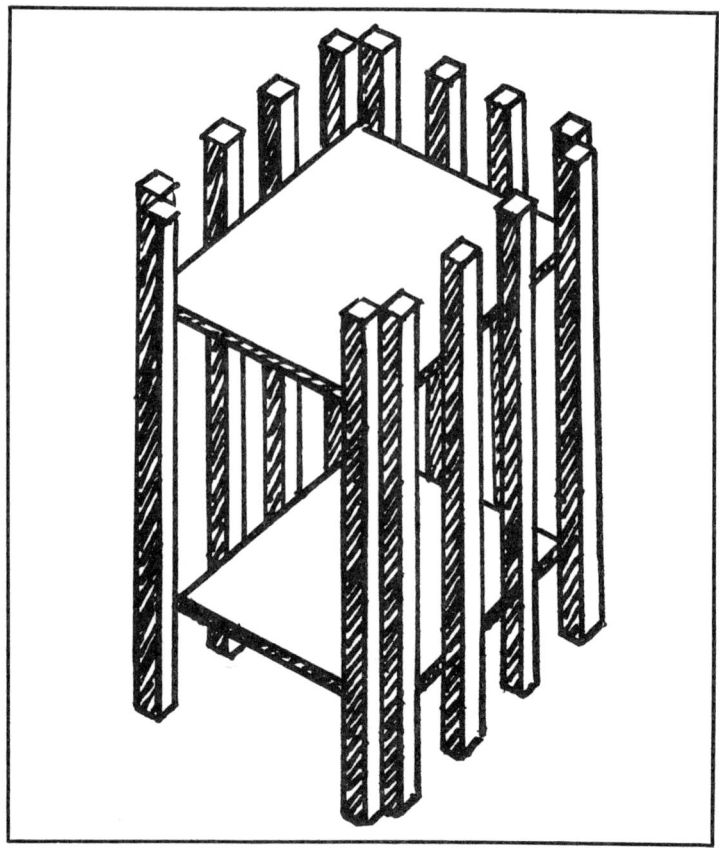

Fig. 1-22. The plant stand has two shelves.

one color. Insert the cord with a tassel on the end through the hole for hanging. (Figs. 1-26 and 1-27).

SAND SCENES

Use an unusual glass container along with the type of sand needed for aquariums. Arrange colored sand in the container using an old cafe rod, skewer or knitting needle. Put ½" of green sand in the bottom, shaking the sand around a bit in a swirling motion. Use the back of a teaspoon and make little waves all the way around the glass on the top of the sand.

Then add a ½" layer of brown sand. Do the same thing with it: then add another ½" of yellow sand for the last layer. You may make the sand garden deeper, depending on the depth of the container.

Fig. 1-23. Pattern for the leather hanging flowerpot holder.

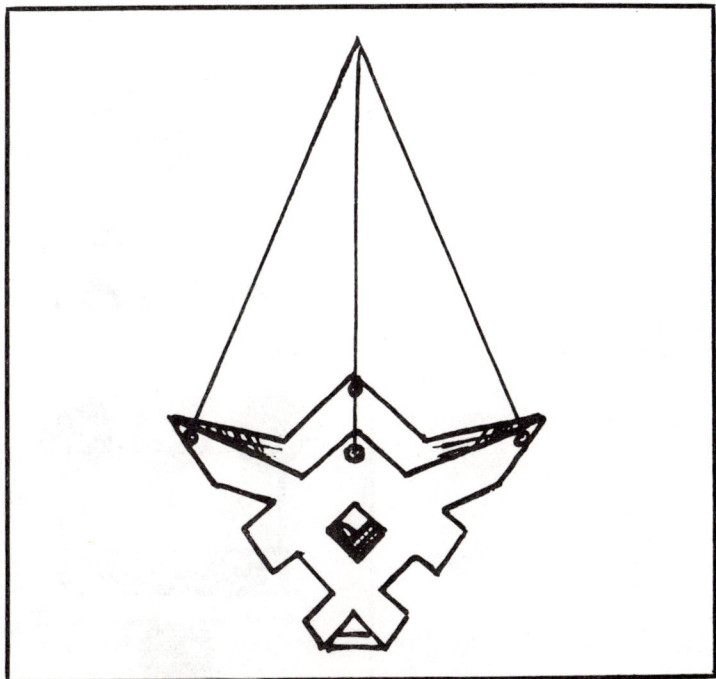

Fig. 1-24. The flowerpot holder is finished and waiting for a plant.

Fig. 1-25. The flower arranging vase.

Take a pencil point and push in against the side of the edge of the glass so different colors of sand will merge.

Take a pencil point and make an indentation in the center. In the hole plant a cactus plant.

Water the garden well and place in a sunny window. Remember, cactus gardens do not need much moisture (Fig. 1-28).

Fig. 1-26. A spool is needed for this project.

Fig. 1-27. Add the tassel and your work is done.

SPONGE GARDEN

Take a kitchen sponge. Wet it and place it in a shallow pan of water. Sprinkle grass seed or any flower or vegetable seeds you wish on the sponge. Be sure to place it in a sunny window and never let it dry out. Sit back and watch your garden grow. Trim the garden if needed (Fig. 1-29).

DRIFTWOOD PLANTER

Find a piece of driftwood on the beach or an old piece of wood from the forest. Decorate it with artificial flowers or berries and greens, depending on the season of the year. In the cracks stick in dried weeds with glue. Glue on acorns, cones and a pretty fabric or ceramic bird. Make a scene on a piece of wood (Fig. 1-30).

MUSHROOM FOR DECORATING PLANTS

Form a mushroom cap from self-hardening clay. Keep it fairly moist by covering with damp cloth while working on the stem.

Fig. 1-28. An attractive sand scene.

Fig. 1-29. Sponge garden.

Form a roll slightly curved for the stem. Make a longer than actual mushroom stem for placing in the ground. It is not necessary to cover the stem as it will not get too dry while you are finishing the cap. On the underside of the cap, use a pencil to make lines to simulate gills. These are the fan-like portions under the cap. Attach the stem with clay paste as in other clay projects. The mushroom may be left the color of clay or dotted on top with brown spots. Push it into the earth in a pot (Fig. 1-31).

GLITTER WALL DECORATION

Use black velvet or *velour* paper 12" × 24". Make a ¾" hem at the top and bottom.

Enlarge the pattern on brown wrapping paper. Since you will be tracing on black, go over the back of the brown paper with chalk or a soft white crayon. Pin to black material and trace. You may have to go over some lines as they may smear a little.

Fig. 1-30. The driftwood planter.

If you cannot find the color of glitter called for, you can mix them as long as they are the same size. Use only one color at a time and spread on large paper while you are working.

Start with the gold. Use a good white glue and spread generously on branches first. Shake on gold glitter and pat with your hand to help it to stick. Allow a few minutes for it to dry. Pick up material and shake the excess off onto paper. Put this back into the container to use again. There is a large area of gold on the tail to cover only a couple of feathers at a time. When all gold is finished, put all excess away and, to avoid mixing colors, use a clean sheet of paper.

Do the turquoise next. Remember, do not try to do too big an area at one time. The glue will sink in and dry, and the glitter will not stick. This means you have to go over it again.

Follow this with the red, violet, yellow and green and finish with the white flowers and bright green leaves. The eye of the feather remains black. The four feathers on the top of the head are a thin gold cord with a small gold bead sewed on the end. Also, use a gold bead for the center of the flowers. The eye is black, beak gold.

Spray paint the dowel sticks gold, and slip them through the top and bottom hems. Tie a black cord around the ends of the top dowel for hanging (Fig. 1-32).

Fig. 1-31. A mushroom for decorating plants.

BRANCHES AND BERRIES PICTURE

Enlarge the pattern onto brown wrapping paper and trace onto a piece of illustration board 30" × 12".

Paint branches and stems a flat black. Buy about one foot of walnut colored contact paper and the same of a maple colored contact paper. Trace the leaves onto the walnut colored contact paper.

You can only trace them on the back of the paper, so you must remember to turn them on the other side so that they will be the right way when cut out. The flowers are traced onto the maple colored contact paper. Cut out all contact paper patterns and apply to the cardboard.

You can use contact paper for the vase or paint it a turquoise color. The berries are cut out of illustration board so that they stand out and are painted a bright red orange. When they are all completed, frame your picture with a narrow walnut frame (Fig. 1-33).

WALL DECORATION OF CHINESE CHARACTERS

Enlarge the pattern as described earlier to make each character 6" or 1" if you prefer. Trace onto illustration board. Cut out with a sharp knife. Make sure all edges are smooth. If they are not, file with emery paper. Paint a flat black. Glue corks to the back where indicated. Attach to the wall with tacky material used to hang pictures (Figs. 1-34 and 1-35).

FLOWER GIRL PICTURE

Collect string, cord and yarn of several colors. Some should be thin, some medium and some fairly thick, but try not to exceed ⅛" in width. Make sure you include black, red, brown, white, yellow, orange, red, blue and two shades of green. The depth of the colors is up to you.

Enlarge the pattern onto a piece of illustration board 12" × 26" (Fig. 1-36). Using poster paints, paint the face and neck a medium brown, like a Tahitian. Leave the whites of the eyes bare. Paint the background a light tan. Try not to cover outlines, eyes, eyebrows, nose, mouth and outline of the bottom of the face.

Figures 1-37 through 1-49 give you many ways to paste the colors on the flowers and leaves, and maybe you can come up with some of your own. Make sure each flower and leaf is almost completely covered with string, yarn or cord. Outline the eyes,

Fig. 1-32. The peacock makes a nice decoration for the wall.

Fig. 1-33. Pattern for the branches and berries picture.

nose, eyelashes and eyebrows with black. The outline of the face can be a dark brown.

The hair is single strands of black yarn and the mouth is red cord. Color the pupil of the eye black and the eyes brown.

When you have completed all cord, yarn and string pasting, frame your picture. It will be a pretty decoration for your room.

LEATHER PICTURE

Enlarge the pattern onto brown wrapping paper and trace onto a medium weight leather of a neutral color. Also trace the duck,

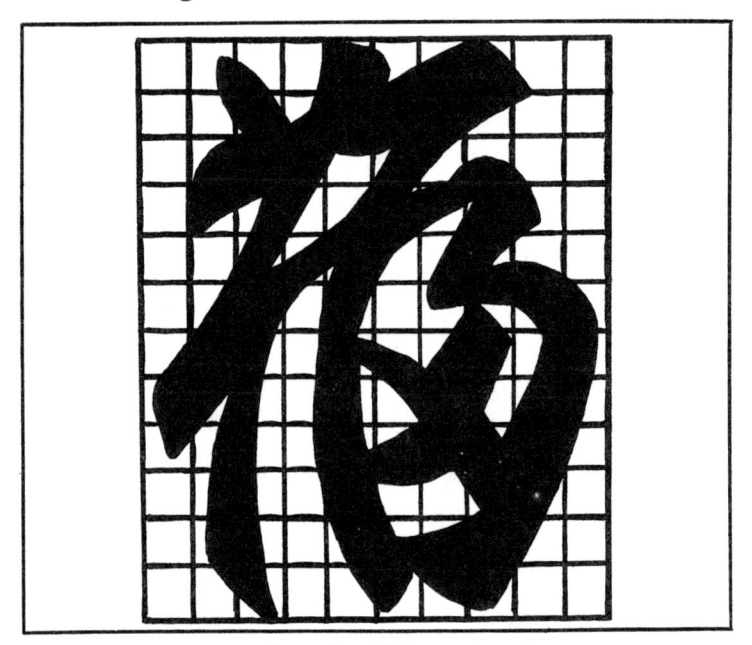

Fig. 1-34. Pattern for a wall decoration of Chinese characters.

38

leaves, stems and cattail, each on a separate piece of the same leather.

Before cementing any pieces on top of the background, use a stain a little darker than the background color and apply around the part of the duck that is above water. Fade it out toward the outside edge of the picture.

Use a green dye and color the water. When both colors are dry, cement the duck in place on the background.

Dampen the leather of the duck with a sponge. Using an orange stick or leather tools, press the lines as they are on the picture, into the leather. Go around the outline of the eye, leaving the eye itself stand out. Outline the feathers. Press the lines that show in the water.

If you wish to color the duck, use stains and paint after the leather has dried.

Cement the leaves and cattail on top of the water. Where one leaf goes over the duck, you will need to use another thickness of the leather under the portion of the leaf that is above and below the duck. This will give you still another dimension.

If you wish to color the leaves and cattail, use leather dyes. Frame your picture with a wooden frame (Fig. 1-50).

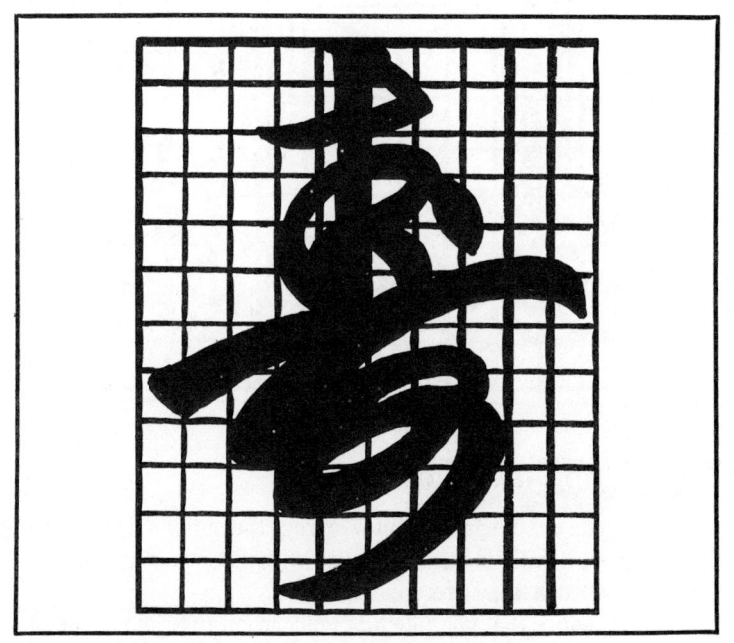

Fig. 1-35. Another Chinese character wall decoration pattern.

Fig. 1-36. Pattern for the flower girl picture.

SMALL PIE PAN PICTURES

Find some old pie pans about 6" across the outside. If they are a little bigger, it will not matter. Polish with steel wool and end up with *Brillo* so that they are clean and shiny.

Find a picture that you like that you can cut to fit the inside of the pan, but not up the sides, and glue to the pan. Drill two holes

40

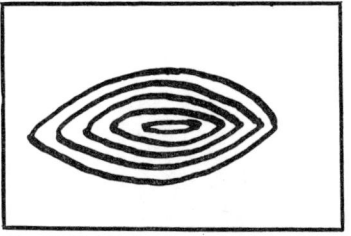

Fig. 1-37. Method of gluing the cord for the leaf.

Fig. 1-38. Method of gluing the cord for the flower.

about ¼" in diameter, where indicated. Run ribbon through the holes in front and tie a bow at the top. You will need to give the pan about two coats of acrylic to keep it shiny.

Another way to decorate the pan is to spray paint both sides with a neutral color. Draw a picture in the center and paint with acrylic paints. This can be followed by a couple of coats of *liquitex gloss* (Fig. 1-51).

CAKE PAN PICTURES

Buy a shallow cake pan in the quarter dollar store, 9 × 13 or smaller. Paint it a flat black.

Use a print or calendar picture or cut one out from a magazine for mounting in the pan. Apply glue on the bottom of the pan and on back of the picture. Paste the print to the inside of the pan.

Let it dry for a day. Then give the complete picture and tin a coat a coat of clear spar varnish.

SILHOUETTE PICTURE

Use regular drawing paper a little larger than you want your picture to be. Wet the paper so that it is damp all over, but not soaking wet. Mix up in small pans red orange, orange, yellow, yellow green, and green water colors so that they are bright and full of water.

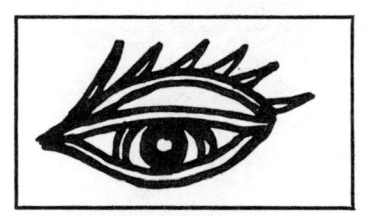

Fig. 1-39. Method of gluing the cord for the eye.

Fig. 1-40. Method of gluing the cord for the lips.

Fig. 1-41. Method of gluing the cord for the leaf.

Fig. 1-42. Method of gluing the cord for another leaf.

If you can place paper on an easel, it will help your colors to flow together. If not, hold the paper with your left hand and, starting at the top with a large brush, brush on red orange. Dip into the orange and brush that on, touching the other so that they run together. Clean your brush and use the yellow next. This should bring you to about the middle of the paper. Wash the brush again and brush on yellow and green. You might want to practice first to see how they run together.

Your green should take you to the bottom of the paper. When thoroughly dry, enlarge the pattern to the size you want and trace onto your colored paper.

Paint the mountains, trees, boat, bushes, wharf and foreground black. Frame your picture with a thin black frame (Fig. 1-52).

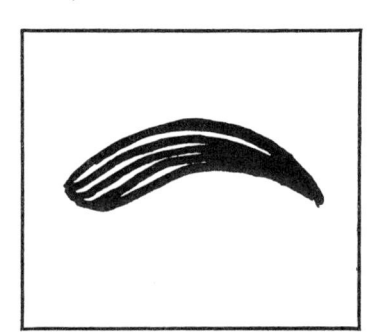

Fig. 1-43. Method of gluing the cord for the eyebrow.

Fig. 1-44. A flower with eight petals.

Fig. 1-45. An interesting flower example.

Fig. 1-46. The flower has 12 sides.

SEASHELL PICTURE

Save paper trays used for fruit or meat that you get from the grocery store. Glue to the inside of the tray tiny seashells that were gathered from the seashore. Use any design that you wish. Label according to name.

Hang up the tray on the wall of your rumpus room. This is a good way to display your collections (Fig 1-53).

WOODEN RINGS PICTURE

Purchase some plain unfinished wooden rings from the quarter dollar store or drapery shop. Paste a round piece of cardboard to a round piece of velvet or felt, using a solid color. Be sure to cut it a little larger than the ring center, and then paste it to the rim of the wooden ring.

Now you are ready to create a picture on this piece of fabric. Find some artificial small flowers, a tiny bird, butterfly or animal.

Fig. 1-47. An attractive flower design.

Fig. 1-48. A star-shaped flower.

Fig. 1-49. Be sure each flower is almost fully covered with cord.

Use a small twig or piece of shrub and arrange your picture around the miniature forest. Glue your materials to the background.

Fasten a small picture frame ring to the back and hang it in your window. It makes a nice Christmas tree decoration (Fig. 1-54).

PENNSYLVANIA DUTCH HEX SIGNS

Make these any size you wish and of any material, such as hardboard or cardboard, depending on the use. The signs will be more appropriate if made small for indoor use and large for outside use.

To copy the designs, you will need to know how to divide a circle into 12 equal parts. This is explained in Chapter 9.

Fig. 1-50. Pattern for the leather picture.

Fig. 1-51. A small pie pan picture.

When you have finished copying the designs, they may be painted with poster paints for indoors or regular enamel or wall paint for outdoors. If you use poster paints, it's a good idea to give them a coat of clear acrylic so they can be cleaned if necessary. The Pennsylvania Dutch like bright colors, so use red, yellow, blue, green and black for accents (Figs. 1-55 and 1-56).

Fig. 1-52. Silhouette picture.

45

Fig. 1-53. Shell picture.

LEOPARD DOORSTOP

Use a large juice bottle and fill it with sand. Glue a cork into the bottle and a 3" rubber ball on top.

Before painting the bottle, use rubber cement and cover the eyes, area around the mouth and open area between legs with paper to fit that section. When these areas are covered, spray paint

Fig. 1-54. Wooden rings picture.

46

Fig. 1-55. Pennsylvania Dutch hex sign.

the bottle and ball with the orange color of a leopard. When the paint is dry, remove the paper and paint these areas white. Paint small spots as indicated with black. Outline eyes, nose, mouth, and leg and paw lines with a black permanent marking pen. Add black pupils to eyes.

Where the ears belong, make a slit wide enough to insert the ears. These are made of the same colored felt as the body of the leopard and lined in front with white felt glued to the other piece. Force glue into the slit and glue the ears in place.

Add a tail of felt from the bottom of the bottle in the back with just enough curl to stick out a little bit. Poke holes with a darning needle along the side of the leopard's nose and glue black bristles from a brush for his whiskers.

If you wish, you can tie a ribbon around his neck or put part of a chain from an old necklace around the neck (Fig. 1-57).

Fig. 1-56. Another Pennsylvania Dutch hex sign.

Fig. 1-57. Leopard doorstop.

MONK DOORSTOP

- Use a rain barrel plastic bottle for body. Paint gray or brown.
- Outline arms as indicated in Fig. 1-58.

Fig. 1-58. Monk doorstop.

48

• Paint a ball for the hands and glue a thin gold cord into the middle to hang about 2".

• Attach a bell. Cover the neck of the bottle with the same colored felt as the body.

• Use a 3" ball for the head. Paint a flesh color.

• Glue movable eyes on and use a cap from a glue bottle or perfume top for the nose.

• Color red. Paint on mouth. Glue felt ears by making a slit first.

• Use fake hair about 1" long and glue around the head as shown. Add cardboard feet.

MIRROR DECORATION

If you have an old plain mirror at home with a frame, remove the frame. If not, you buy one at the five and ten—about 9" × 18" is a good size.

Trace the shape of your mirror onto brown wrapping paper and sketch designs at the top and one side. You can use the one in Fig. 1-59 or make up your own. When you have a design you like which does not take up more than 2" off all sides of the mirror, trace it onto the mirror with carbon paper. Make the two sides the same and the top and bottom the same.

Paint the designs with glass paint. Outline with a black permanent marking pen.

LARGE FRUITCAKE CAN REDECORATED

The decoration shown in Fig. 1-60 is one that has been hand painted. If you wish to do yours this way, you will have to measure

Fig. 1-59. Mirror decoration.

Fig. 1-60. Top view of the large redecorated fruitcake can.

the diameter of the lid and make a circle that size on a piece of paper. Following the directions for making the hex signs, divide your circle into 12 equal parts. Draw the inner circles and copy the design onto paper.

To find out how many hearts you will need for around the can, measure around the can with a strip of paper that just meets. Fold this strip in half, then in half again, and keep folding until each section is the size you want it to be. Draw one heart on one section and trace as many as you need to go around the can.

Spray paint your can whatever color you wish, both the lid and sides. If you use a dark color, you will have to trace the designs on with chalk. If a light color is used, you can use carbon paper.

Carefully paint each part of the designs with a liquitex paint. Make sure you use a flat spray paint for the can. Then the whole can can be given a coat of acrylic spray.

If this seems too hard for you, glue a picture to the top of the can after it is colored. For the sides, you can use cutouts and braid or rickrack around the top and bottom edges (Fig. 1-61).

A SMALL SCREEN

Enlarge the pattern onto brown wrapping paper and trace onto illustration board. Cut out the outline. Indicate the dotted lines since that is where you will score the cardboard to make it fold easier.

Fig. 1-61. Side view of the redecorated fruitcake can.

Paint the tree trunk and all branches a dark brown, the plum blossoms pink, the foreground green, and the mountains a lavender mixed with a little brown to tone the color down a little. Color the boats brown, with yellow roofs, and outline the lines with a thin, black permanent ink pen. Paint the margins black.

With a sharp knife cut out all water and sky areas. Behind this cutout area of water and sky, paste a turquoise blue tissue paper or cellophane for the water and a pale blue for the sky. You can, if you wish, cover the other side with a frame like the front to cover the tissue paper with just black paper (Fig. 1-62).

STENCILED PLACE MATS

To stencil this design, you will find it easier to use a clear plastic lid rather than stencil paper. You will be using permanent marking pens to color them.

Fig. 1-62. Small screen.

Butcher linen makes a very good material for place mats. Buy enough for as many mats as you wish to make. Each should be 11" × 16". Stitch around the edge of each with a zigzag stitch or double line of plain stitching, 1" in from the edge. Fray from there out.

Now you are ready to make your stencil. For the large design in the middle, use a coffee can lid or whipped cream lid of clear plastic. Enlarge both patterns. To trace them onto plastic lids, you will find it easier to scotch tape your design to the underside and go over the lines with a sharp pointed tool like a darning needle or ice pick.

When both patterns have been traced, cut out the white areas with a sharp knife, but do not cut out the outline. Pin your place mat to a board with a blotter between the material and the board. Now pin your plastic stencil wherever you feel it needs to be held taut.

With a red permanent colored marking pen, fill in the open spaces. Stencil the large one in the center and the smaller one in each of the corners. When that is completed, use a ruler and draw a line with a black permanent colored pen between the ones in each corner (Figs 1-63 and 1-64).

BRAIDED MATS

Cut strips of woolen or cotton fabric 1" wide. Use three colors, two plaids and a solid or whatever color scheme you choose. Roll one color into a ball. Continue until you have three balls of fabric.

Take three strands from each ball and sew together at the top. Start to braid like you would a girl's pigtail by hand. Be sure to carefully turn under the raw edges on both sides as these mats are reversible. You can buy in the yarn shops three metal rug braids that can be attached to the strands and turn automatically as you braid.

Make a coil of the braid and go round and round in a circle or oval shape, and set together with heavy button thread. Try to keep the coil flattened out when sewing it fast (Fig. 1-65).

HAIR SPRAY COVER-UP

Use an empty hair spray can. Cut some scrap material to fit around the can, leaving ¼" for overlapping.

Now wrap the can up in the material and glue around the edges of the overlap. If you are using solid color material, you can cut out the designs and glue them to the material. Decorating with sequins and old beads makes an attractive cover-up.

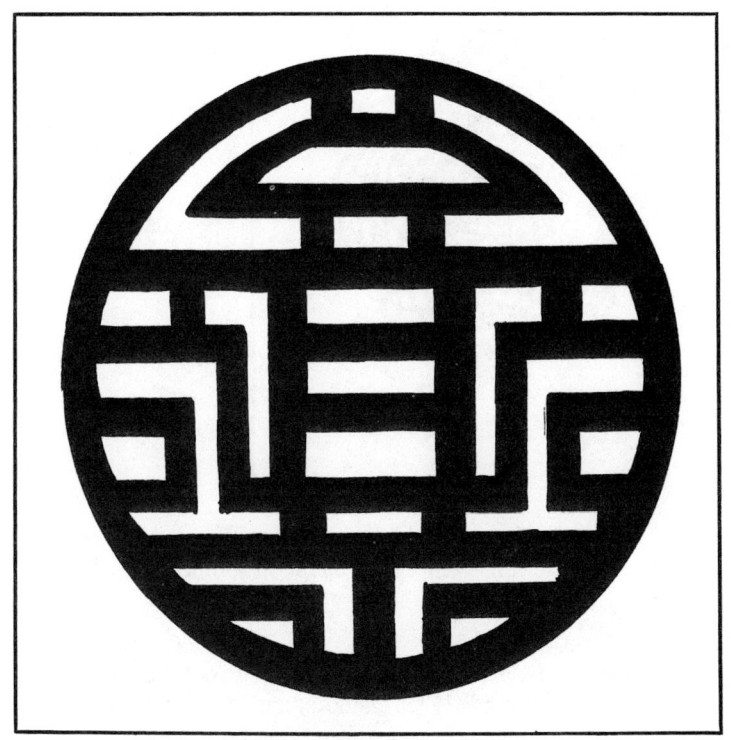

Fig. 1-63. Center design for the stenciled place mat.

Fig. 1-64. Corner design for the stenciled place mat.

Fig. 1-65. Braided mat.

Be sure to let the cover dry before using. You can slip off this cover-up when the can is empty and use it on another (Fig. 1-66).

GOURD ASHTRAY

Cut a hole in one side of the *gourd*. Clean out well. Cut two holes on the opposite side ½" in diameter and one in the front of the gourd about ¼".

Paint the gourd to suit your taste as you would like a bird to look. If you can obtain a coconut shell, it would be a good size for

Fig. 1-66. Hair spray cover-up.

the head; if not, you will have to use a very light piece of wood about 4" × 6" and shape according to Fig. 1-67. Paint the eye and beak and drill a hole (small) to insert a pipe cleaner—a large, thick one for his neck.

Use about ⅜" dowel sticks for legs. Cut a circle from ½" thick wood for the base and glue the dowels in the base. Drill a few very small holes in the head and tail and insert colored feathers.

CORK COASTERS

Cut two 3" circles from inch cork sheeting. Cut out a 2¼" circle from the middle.

On the solid circle paint one side white with acrylic paints. Trace from a deck of cards the heart in the center of the ace, club,

Fig. 1-67. Gourd ashtray.

spade and diamond. Trace these onto the white surface and paint red or black according to the original color.

Cut one 3" circle from acetate and glue on it the top of the white side. Glue only around the edge.

Glue the other cork ring on top. You will need four full circles and four rings to complete a set (Fig. 1-68).

BUTTERFLY MOBILE

- Enlarge the butterfly pattern. Trace on lightweight cardboard for the pattern. Use acetate for butterflies. Trace the pattern with a sharp tool and cut out.
- Color each of five butterflies with marking pens on both sides. Fold in the middle and open to represent flight.
- Glue a thin black pipe cleaner on top for the body. Use a nylon brush bristle for the antenna and glue under the body.
- Pierce the butterfly in the center with a needle and thread a knot at the bottom, leaving long thread to tie onto the hanger. The hanger may be made from piano wire or ¼" dowel sticks. If wire, cut four pieces of 4" and bend to a curve. With pliers, make a small circle at each end to which you tie the butterfly.
- Cross wires, glue and tie in the middle. Tie the thread to the center and hang to assemble. If you are using dowels, use two 3" × ¼" dowels, tie and cross in the center. Hang butterflies at various lengths and one in the middle. They are easier to balance when hanging (Figs. 1-69 and 1-70).

CLAY TRIVET

Roll out self-hardening clay on the wrong side of oil cloth with a rolling pin until a uniform thickness of about ½", large enough to cut out a hexagon 6" across (Fig. 1-71).

Allow the clay to dry a little so that when you cut into it, the clay will cut clean but not thoroughly dry; trace a design on with an orange stick by pressing lines, but not deep. Cut out white areas and outline.

Form three balls of the same clay approximately ½" in size. Mix a little of the clay with water to form a paste and adhere these balls where indicated. Allow to thoroughly dry. Smooth clay with emery paper and paint both sides with enamel (Fig. 1-72).

CHEESE BOX OTTOMAN

Get a large old fashioned round cheese box about 16" in diameter and 14" deep. Buy a round flat (about 2" foam pillow as

Fig. 1-68. Cork coasters.

close to the diameter of the lid as you can get). If it is too large, the pillow can be cut down. It must reach across the lid.

Select material like *velveteen* or velour that has a body to it and is at least 20" or more wide. You will need enough to go around the box with an overlap of about an inch and reaching from the top of the box and under about 2", plus enough to cover the top of the lid with the pillow on and to cover the sides of the lid.

Fig. 1-69. Butterfly mobile design.

Fig. 1-70. The assembled butterfly mobile.

Trace the top of the box onto brown wrapping paper and add the size of the depth of the pillow and sides to it. Cut out, pin on material and cut.

Fig. 1-71. Top view of the clay trivet.

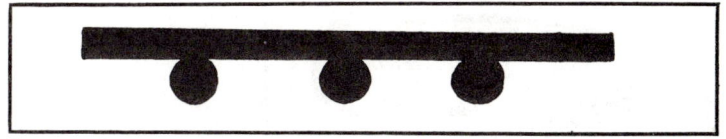

Fig. 1-72. Side view of the clay trivet.

Measure the distance around the box, plus at least 1" for overlapping and as deep as the box plus 2". Cut out the material and glue around the side of the box. Turn the extra over at the bottom of the box. You will have to make folds in it so that it will remain flat. Glue to the bottom of the box. To complete the bottom, you cut a circle of the same material or another, if you think that will be big enough to cover over the bottom of the box, leaving about 1" of the turned under material showing. Staple this piece on the bottom around the edge.

To cover the top of the box, glue the pillow onto the lid. When the glue is dry, cover with the material you cut for the lid, folding it over occasionally on the side of the lid to make it lay as flat as it can. To complete your ottoman, sew a wide braid around the edge of the lid. It becomes an ottoman with two purposes. You can store things in it as well as rest your feet on it (Fig. 1-73).

SMOKING STAND

Cut a circle 18" in diameter from ½" hardboard. Cut another circle 12" in diameter from ¾" hardboard. These circles will be the top and bottom of your smoking stand. Scout around in the attic and secondhand stores until you find a fancy table leg. You may have to buy the whole table to get the leg, but if you do you've got the beginnings of two more smoking stands.

Fig. 1-73. Cheese box ottoman.

Fig. 1-74. Smoking stand.

Sand off all the covering down to the bare wood. Sand the edges of the circles so that they are smooth.

Buy a small ashtray from the five and ten store if you do not have one. Get one that has a ledge on it. Cut a circle out of the larger one so that the ashtray will fit into it, the ledge keeping it from falling through (Fig. 1-74).

Now you are ready to assemble the stand. Use two screws ⅞"-2"-½". Drill a hole to start screws in the center of both the large and small circles. Screw a large circle into the center of the table leg at one end and the small circle to the bottom. Countersink the screws. By *countersinking,* you screw them in lower than the surface of the wood. Fill with plastic wood and smooth.

Paint the entire stand flat black. Give two coats. Enlarge and trace the design onto the top. Paint with gold. Also, paint a few strips around the leg. If you do not want a flat color, use enamel; but gold will take better on the flat. Insert the ashtray.

CURTAIN ROOM DIVIDER

Ask your friends to save the plastic ring from scotch tape spools. Decide how many you will need to reach from the top of the door to the floor using 2" large plastic or wooden balls between each one. Measure the width of the door, and depending on how close you want them to be, multiply by how many you need for the length. This will tell you how many spools you will need altogether, and how many beads.

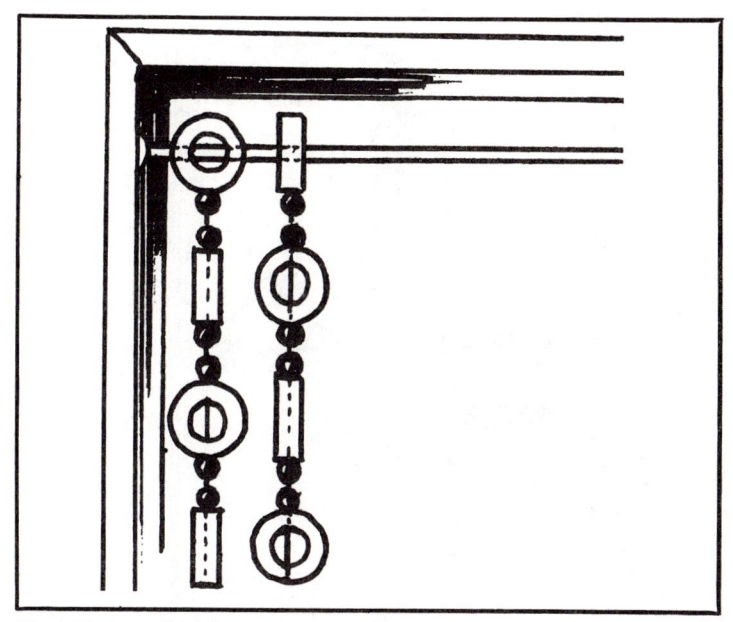

Fig. 1-75. Assembly of the curtain room divider.

Drill a ⅜" hole from side through the other of the spools you will need to go across the top of the door. Drill ⅛" holes from one side of all the spools through to the other side, with the exception of those that will go across the top. In those drill the ⅛" hole only through one side. A bead on the inside of the top spool will then hold the cord for the rest of them.

You will find it easier to first tie the cord you intend to use to hang the spools inside the top spool. If you hang the rod up first, it will be easier to work and not get tangled. After the first spool is

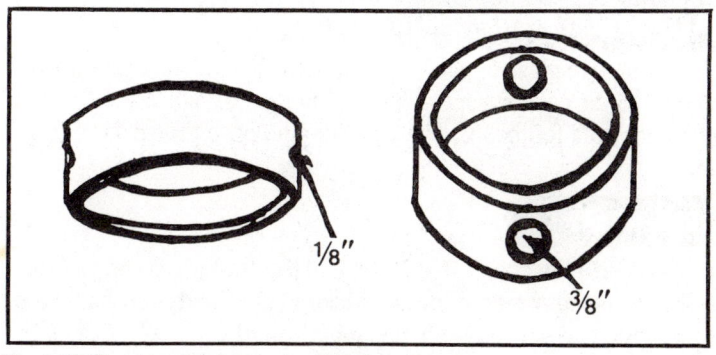

Fig. 1-76. Curtain room divider showing separate coils.

Fig. 1-77. Salt and pepper shakers.

hung on the rod, start adding the balls and a spool. Then add two more balls and a spool until you reach the bottom. You can end off with a spool or larger bead if you desire. Continue with each string the same way (Figs. 1-75 and 1-76).

SALT AND PEPPER SHAKERS

Take two glass or plastic pill bottles about 3" tall. Cover with wood grained contact paper. Spray paint the lid gold. Trace "S" and "P" onto gold foil paper. Cut out and glue onto the shakers (Fig. 1-77).

WOODEN TRAY

Cut ¼" plywood, 18" × 12" round the corners as shown (Fig. 1-78). For handles, get 6" dowel sticks 1" thick and cut in half. Saw a ¼" slot halfway through the length of the dowel stick. Get someone who knows woodworking to chisel that piece out as

Fig. 1-78. Wooden tray.

shown in Fig. 1-78. You will probably have to sand the space a little to make it fit over the ends of the tray for handles. Glue these on. Either paint a design on your tray or find a particular picture that you like. Glue it on the center of the tray.

You can paint the rest of the tray whatever color you wish or stain with a wood stain. Spray with clear acrylic, or paint with waterproof varnish.

WASTEPAPER BASKET MAGIC

Find an old wastepaper basket. Sand it well, inside and outside. Paint it with a colored enamel, using a different shade for the inside.

Fig. 1-79. Decorate the wastebasket with colored pictures.

Fig. 1-80. Palm tree refrigerator stickup.

When the can is dry, decorate it with colored cutout pictures; if you are handy with a brush, paint on your own designs. Brush on a spar varnish inside and outside (Fig. 1-79).

REFRIGERATOR STICKUPS

Trace the designs onto thin cardboard and one piece of felt. Use felt of the color you want your design to be. Cut out cardboard and felt. Glue the felt to the cardboard. You can buy magnets in one strip. Cut off a piece the size you need and adhere to the back of the cardboard (Figs. 1-80 through 1-83).

Fig. 1-81. Poinsettia refrigerator stickup.

Fig. 1-82. Duck refrigerator stickup.

GOURDS ON A BRAID

Harvest or buy small gourds with a stem, known as the *calabash*. Dry them thoroughly. When you hear the seeds rattle, they are ripe. Varnish or shellac them well and let dry.

Make a braid using three lengths of fabric 3′ long. Tie a braid of fabric or twine around one gourd stem. Leave a space of 3″ and tie another one until you have five or six gourds on the braid. Hang up against the kitchen wall on a cup hook (Fig. 1-84).

POT HOLDERS

Cut pieces of homespun 6″ × 6″ square. Hem up three sides.

Stuff the pot holder with scraps of material until it looks like a small cushion but is still usable to grip a kettle handle. Sew up the

Fig. 1-83. Butterfly refrigerator stickup.

65

Fig. 1-84. Gourds on a braid.

fourth opening and attach a bone hook by sewing it to a corner for hanging (Fig. 1-85).

HANDLE HOLDER

Cut small pieces of fabric 6" long by 4" wide. Sew to this a heavy lining using the same measurements. Fold it lengthwise and sew up three sides, leaving one of the short ends open. Stick this on your kettle handles and save burned hands (Fig. 1-86).

TRAY FUN

Use an old tray with a glass top or a picture frame. Remove glass, and paste colored construction paper or felt cut to size on back of the tray or frame.

Arrange pretty dried leaves and glue around the edge. Use a leaf with an interesting surface. You can use ferns and wild and garden flowers for the design.

Fasten leaves with clear glue to paper or felt. Place a heavy weight like a magazine or book over the design for a few days.

Before you replace glass on the tray or picture frame, you can melt paraffin or beeswax around the edges of glass to seal tightly to the tray. Place the glass on top. This makes an unusual and practical tray (Fig. 1-87).

PAPER NAPKIN HOLDER

Cut a toilet paper roll about 2½" long. Cut with a knife so it does not crush. Cut a piece of contact paper ½" longer than the roll.

Adhere to the roll leaving ¼" at end. Cut this extra piece or slit at intervals and fold inside. Paint the inside first, the same color as contact paper. Use ½" braid to glue around the top, half inside and half outside (Fig. 1-88).

BIRCH BARK NAPKIN HOLDER

Cut a slab of soft wood about 1½" wide from a small log from the woods. Birch makes a beauty.

Take a small chisel and hammer or use a brace and bit and gouge out the center carefully. Sand all rough edges.

Fig. 1-85. A homespun pot holder.

Fig. 1-86. A pot handle holder.

If you are using just plain wood, you can carve your initials in the wood. Apply a coat of spar varnish to preserve the holder (Fig. 1-89).

ETCHED GLASS

Any drinking glass will do to make an imitation snow glass design. Trace the pattern onto typewriting paper and cut out black areas. Leave about ½" margin all around the design.

Use rubber cement and glue the pattern to the glass. Make sure the edges are down tight. Also, make sure all traces of rubber cement are off the area to be etched.

Get the glass etching material. Apply to the open area as directed on the tube. Follow directions for the length of time to leave etching material on.

When time is up, wash the etching solution off with water and dry the glass. If any cement is still adhering, rub it off with your fingers. (Figs. 1-90 and 1-91).

STRING POT

Take an empty coffee can and at the bottom (closed end) spread some glue. Then wind ordinary twine around and around the outside of the can.

Fig. 1-87. This tray is unusual and practical.

You will find that a small bit of glue holds the ends of the twine at the bottom. On reaching the top of the can, fasten the loose end of twine or string with glue, holding it in place with a clothespin until it is thoroughly dry.

Use a clear coat of shellac to make the pot shine. A string pot may be used as a planter, pencil holder or as a catch-all (Fig. 1-92).

Fig. 1-88. Paper napkin holder.

Fig. 1-89. Birch bark napkin holder.

RATTAN BASKET

If you live near a grove of willow trees, cut off the young thin shoots. Scrape off the bark until clean. Soak them in a bucket of water to keep them pliable.

Fig. 1-90. Glass etching design.

Fig. 1-91. The glass is very attractive.

Make a braided flat coil with the willow roots, sewing them together with *raffia* or *rattan* that you will find in a hobby shop. The Indians sewed the willow roots together with pieces of bark from the tree using a big eyed needle made from the bone of a deer's leg.

Fig. 1-92. The string jar has a variety of uses.

Fig. 1-93. The rattan basket bottom.

Whenever you add a new shoot, cut both the old piece and the new piece to a long point so there will be no bump on an overlap. Then the next coil of shoots are laid on flat but raised a little. Weave until the walls of the basket are four fingers high.

To make the basket colorful, collect red berries or the inkberries and crush them to make a dye. Soak some of the shoots in the dye and weave your last round in red, which in Indian life means good luck. Fasten by slipping the last end of the shoot under other shoots. You may buy raffia and rattan in a hobby shop to create your basket if you have no willow trees available. (Figs. 1-93 and 1-94).

TIN CAN OR TIN CAN LID COASTERS

If you use a tin can, get one about the size of a tuna fish can. Spray paint inside and out after smoothing out the edge.

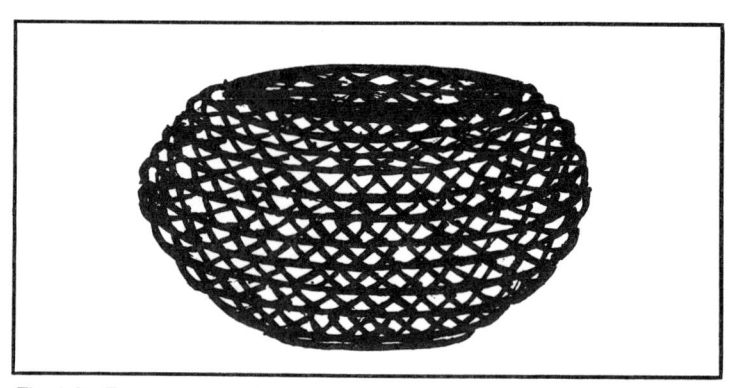

Fig. 1-94. The rattan basket sides.

Fig. 1-95. Tin can coasters.

One way to decorate this kind is to saw fairly large wooden balls in half. Using a rasp or file, file the flat side a little curved so that it will fit the side of the can all around the edge of the bead. You will need about six or eight, depending on the size of the bead.

If you wish the beads to be colored other than they are, you must paint them before you glue them on. Glue them on slightly below the middle of the can and glue braid around the top edge.

If you decide to use a lid for the coaster, fill the lid to about ¼" of the top with plaster. Let the plaster set. Give the plaster a coat of *liquitex matte* paint to seal the plaster.

Fig. 1-96. Paint your house number on the yard sign.

73

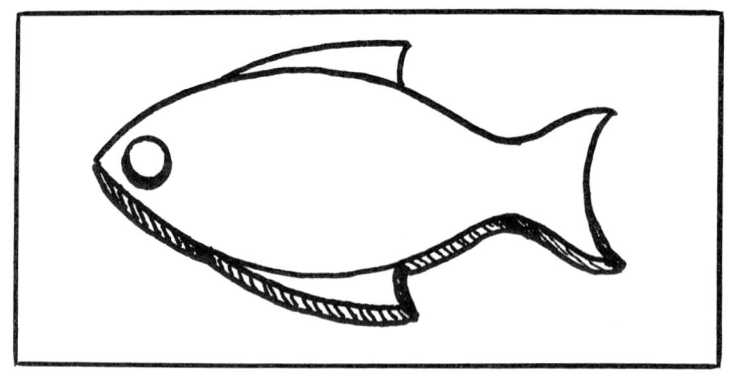

Fig. 1-97. A fish-shaped cutting board.

Cut out of paper or paint a heart, diamond, spade and club. Glue to the center of each one or paint in the center of each one. You can now use a clear acrylic on top or liquitex gloss. (Fig. 1-95).

YARD SIGN

Find a piece of scrap wood ¾" thick. And another piece of 2 × 4 wood for the post which should measure 2 feet long. Be sure to cut a slant on the bottom of the board so it will go into the ground easily.

Round the corners of the sign board or leave them square. Nail the board to the top of the 2 × 4 post. Be sure to have it in the

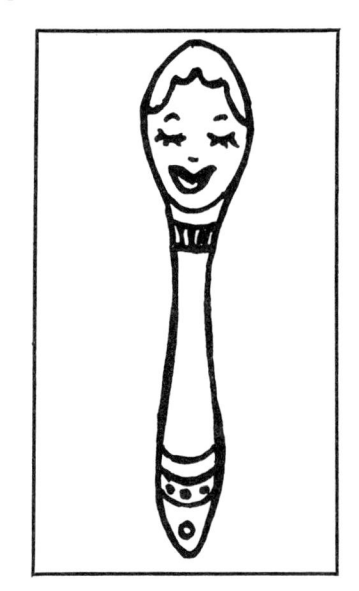

Fig. 1-98. The painted wooden spoon.

74

Fig. 1-99. Shell centerpiece.

center. Paint the boards with two coats of outside paint. When dry, paint your house number or name in black letters or numbers (Fig. 1-96).

Fig. 1-100. Give your bathroom a new look.

Fig. 1-101. Shadow box.

CUTTING BOARD

A good cutting board will save your counter tops from becoming soiled and scratched. Use a very hard wood such as maple, oak or ash. You will need a jigsaw. Enlarge the pattern so that your cutting board is approximately 15" × 12". Transfer the design to the wood.

After it has been cut out and the hole drilled for the eye, use sandpaper from coarse to fine. Clean off all the edges and the inside of the hole. Go over one side only with a good waterproof varnish and hang it in the kitchen where it will be handy (Fig. 1-97).

WOODEN SPOON DECOR

Purchase a wooden spoon at the quarter dollar store. Draw and paint with enamels a lady's or man's face in the hollow of the spoon. You can glue in the hollow, small artificial flowers.

Tie a bright colored ribbon around the end of the handle. Hang it on a hook on the kitchen wall (Fig. 1-98).

CONCH SHELL

Use a conch shell and clean it well. Anchor it on an attractive plate with floristic clay. Fill it with the flowers from your garden. Be sure to water everyday. Place a candle ring around the plate to fancy up the shell.

If you wish to plant a live plant in the shell, place good soil in the bottom and plant an ivy in the shell. Covering the soil with a piece of moss keeps the earth moist. Place the shell on a plate and use it on a coffee table or mantel (Fig. 1-99).

RE-DOING AN OLD BATHROOM SINK

Do you have an old bathroom sink with the pipes hanging out? Find a wooden wash stand. Cut out the top and slip it under the old sink. You will find when you open the little door below that you have a place for your wash cloths and towels.

You may want to revarnish it to give it a new look. It is an inexpensive way to pep up your old bathroom (Fig. 1-100).

OLD DOUGH BOX

Sand the box down and rub it down with *linseed oil,* or use a heritage clear varnish. Under the lid you may store your linens. On the top of the box you can place a lamp. Practical and lovely, it is an antique to grace your living room.

SHADOW BOX

Here's a good autumn project. Find an old picture frame. Remove the back and build out 2" with plywood. Tack the back on a new extension.

Fig. 1-102. Key hanger.

Fig. 1-103. Popsicle trellis.

Varnish the extension to match the frame, inside and outside. On the inside of the frame, draw a design or use your own imagination for the picture.

Gather dried weeds by the wayside. Arrange them in an attractive manner on the inside of the frame. Be sure to use the tall

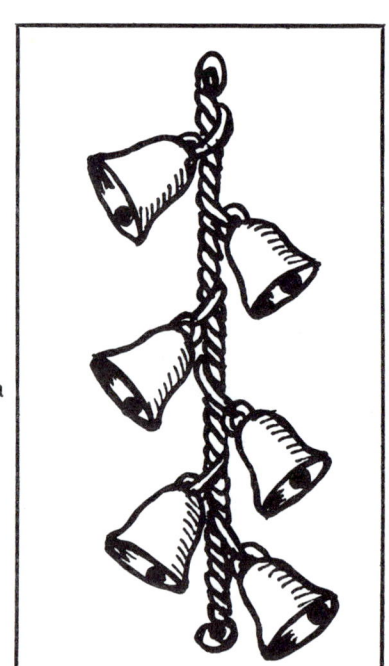

Fig. 1-104. String the door bells on a cord.

78

Fig. 1-105. The sit-upon makes a nice cushion.

weeds in the background and the smaller ones up front. When you have them arranged the way you wish, secure them by tacking carefully small staples that have been dipped in brown paint. Try to staple under foilage to cover the staples. If you wish to close the picture in glass, it will remain clean and protected (Fig. 1-101).

KEY HANGER

Take a piece of barn wood and screw in cup hooks. Hang up your keys. Hang a hook on the back of the board for easy hanging in the kitchen.

Fig. 1-106. The completed cookie cutter holder.

Fig. 1-107. Nail keg stool.

If you wish to make your own barnwood, you can buy inexpensive pieces of leftovers in the lumber mill. Take them home and use a hard wire brush to scrape over the wood. Do this a few times so the wood looks worn. Then chisel out small slivers of wood with a screwdriver driven by your hammer. Take a candle and light it. Place the board into the flame every few inches. Then use the wire brush again to get the effect. Some folks give the new lumber an antique look by using an antique kit. After painting the wood, use a wire brush and notch every now and then (Fig. 1-102).

Fig. 1-108. Nail keg lamp.

POPSICLE TRELLIS FOR A PLANT

Wash the popsicle sticks well and dry thoroughly. Glue two together on top of each other for firmness.

Overlap two double thickness of sticks and glue together with a strong glue. The upright sticks are the only ones that are double thickness.

Glue evenly on the uprights some popsicle sticks. These will be the cross sticks. Be sure to space them evenly.

Arrange the upright sticks so they will taper down and fit into the pot. This little inexpensive trellis is good to support a trailing vine (Fig. 1-103).

DOOR BELLS

Purchase some large bells that can be strung on a cord. You will find them in a craft shop.

Choose at least six of them. Knot them at intervals on a strong ornamental cord that you will find in a fabric store in the trimming department.

Leave a loop at the top of the cord and hang them up on the inside of your front door. You will always be aware of a visitor (Fig. 1-104).

SIT-UPON

Cut a piece of vinyl fabric 12" × 12" square. On the wrong side, stitch up three sides.

Turn to the right side of the article and stuff with foam particles or a piece of foam using the third side. Stitch up the third side securely.

Fig. 1-109. Marble top table.

Fig. 1-110. This step ladder holds plants.

On the top of the sit-upon, paint initials or a design to make it attractive. The sit-upon makes a good cushion for an outdoor picnic (Fig. 1-105).

SHELF COVERING

Purchase a plastic tablecloth and cut to size according to the measurement of the shelves. Fasten the fabric to the shelves by tacking it to the wood with thumbtacks.

SCRUBBERS

Purchase some remnants of heavy net that will hold its shape. Cut squares 6" × 6" square.

Lay everything out on a table and in the center of the square place pieces of cut-up net to make a ball as large as a plum. Tie around the ball and tie net with a strong cord. Trim off the ends of the cord. This simple little article is a great scrubber for pots and pans.

BARN LUMBER BOOKCASE

You may need a bookcase in your home, and lumber is so expensive. If you live in the country and somebody lets you tear an be old building down, consider it a treasure. All of that lumber can used to make interesting gifts for your home.

For the bookcase, cut the long pieces of lumber 47" long. These will be your sides. You will need two of them. Then cut two pieces 34" long. These will be the shelves. You will need four shelves and will have to use two widths of the barn boards if they do not measure 7½" wide. You may have to add or subtract the measurements because of the old barn wood.

Take the two sides and nail in the shelves 10¼" apart (this will be the measurement of three shelves). The top shelf used for large books will measure 12" with 3" between shelves.

There will be a top shelf for extra books or knickknacks. This bookcase will be a floor model.

BARN LUMBER COOKIE CUTTER HOLDER

Choose a piece of barn lumber that will measure 12" wide and 24" long. You may have to use two pieces of wood from the old lumber. If you wish, tack a piece of molding around the wood for effect.

Attach antique cookie cutters onto the board by using small hooks or nails. If you do not have antique cookie cutters, you can use the new ones on the market and tint them with a metal paint to make them look old.

Attach a hook at the back of the board. Hang it in your kitchen as a conversation piece (Fig. 1-106).

PICTURE FRAMES

Using old barn lumber, cut wood according to your picture measurement. Miter the corners and fasten with *chevrons*. Choose a piece of wood for the backing. Insert the picture and cover with glass using push points to hold the glass. Attach a hook on the back of the frame for hanging.

KITCHEN TABLE

Find an old dining room tabletop in a secondhand shop. Take it home and sand it down, filling any cracks with tinted plastic wood. Give the top a coat of heritage clear varnish or rub down with linseed oil.

For the base, use an old treadle sewing machine bottom which is made of cast iron. Remove the wooden top and clamp the base to the tabletop with heavy bolts or screws.

Your dining guests will enjoy looking down under the table and seeing the word SINGER on the treadle which will still move. This is a way to save money and have a practical and attractive table in your kitchen.

NAIL KEG STOOLS AND LAMP HOLDERS

At flea markets and garage sales or old country stores, you can find an old nail keg. Clean it well and paint or varnish the base.

Set the keg with the open end on the floor. On the top of the keg fit a piece of rubber foam. Take a strong piece of material and fit it tightly over the foam and tack around the keg. Where tacks show, cover with a bright colored braid and fasten the ends together.

Nail kegs can be used as stools in recreation rooms and children's rooms. For lamp holders, paint or varnish the top of the keg to match. Set the lamp on top for a lamp table (Figs. 1-107 and 1-108).

MARBLE TOP TABLE

Find a wooden base from an old table at a garage sale or secondhand shop. Visit the tombstone cutter with the base and measure out a piece of marble to fit. Clamp the marble to the base with clamps from the hardware store. If the marble is very heavy, you can lay it on the base of the table. This table may be used for a lamp table or coffee table.

Another type of marble table may be made by hunting a piece of marble that has a rectangular shape. Attach heavy wooden legs built on a wooden base to hold the marble to the table top. Clamp or sit the marble on top of the wooden base. This makes an attractive serving table for a living room (Fig. 1-109).

STEP LADDER FUN

Buy a small wooden step ladder in the hardware store. Paint it white. Cover it with a spar varnish.

Place it in your dining room, and on the steps place your favorite potted plants. The very small ladders do not take up as much room and fit into a corner of a room if you have a small house (Fig. 1-110).

Chapter 2
Personalized Gifts

Gift giving should be pleasant, but it can become a burden, especially the cost. Save yourself a little money and time spent hunting for gifts that are just right. Make them yourself.

From the variety of things in this chapter, you should be able to find something to fit everyone on your list, including those with the most fastidious tastes. All are inexpensive and easy enough for anyone to make. You will also be giving a gift that will be one of a kind and one that you might never have been able to purchase (Fig. 2-1).

CLOVER LEAF JEWELRY

Hunt for a four leaf clover. Take two rubber jar rings. Paste a circle of transparent white paper that is cut to fit the circle on the inner side of one jar ring.

Paste a four leaf clover in the center of the paper circle. Paste a circle of clear wrapping paper to the inner side of the second ring. Paste the two rings together with your clover leaf inside. Punch a hole at the top and hang it from a gold ribbon (Fig. 2-2).

BRASS WIRE PIN

Start with a piece of brass wire about 15 or 16 gauge. With pliers and file, make one end into a point for a pin. Bend the wire to form the shape in Fig. 2-3. When bending is complete, using a hammer, flatten the wire where it is wider.

Use sandpaper and steel wool to erase hammer marks and polish with metal cleaner. This is a stick pin or scarf pin.

Fig. 2-1. Make some inexpensive personalized gifts.

WOODEN BIRD OR FLOWER PIN

Find an old branch from a tree that has broken off about 1½" in diameter. Have someone cut a slice no thicker than ¼" and on an angle. Sand front and back with sandpaper to make smooth. Leave the bark on.

Find a picture from a seed catalog or magazine that you like: trace a shape of wood onto it and cut out. Glue this on one side of the wood. Make sure no paper sticks out over the edge. If it does, do some trimming. Give both sides of the pin about two or three coats of liquitex gloss. Glue the pin back to back (Fig. 2-4).

JEWELRY FROM PULL-OFF CAPS OF METAL CANS

The pull-off tabs from coffee cans make excellent pendants, necklaces or charm bracelet (Figs. 2-5 through 2-7). Pull off the

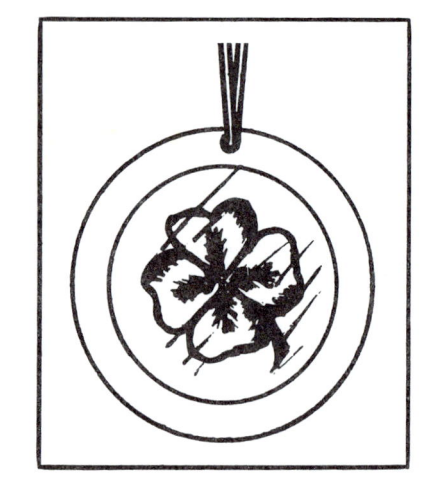

Fig. 2-2. Clover leaf jewelry.

Fig. 2-3. Brass wire pin.

small ring that usually breaks when the cap is pulled off. Smooth the edge if necessary with emery paper.

If you just want to make a pendant, drill a hole big enough to take a fairly large jump ring where shown in Fig. 2-5. Collect the beads in graduating sizes or four small ones and one large one. Starting at the bottom, tie a knot to a piece of thread that is long enough to go through all beads to be used with enough left over to tie another knot. Thread the largest bead and then the next four. Go through the hole you drill to the back and through the beads again to the large one at the bottom. Tie thread to that knot and cut as close as possible. Place your jump ring through the same hole and over your chain.

If you want several to hang on the chain, make sure the links are large enough for the jump ring to go through these links at

Fig. 2-4. Wooden bird pin.

87

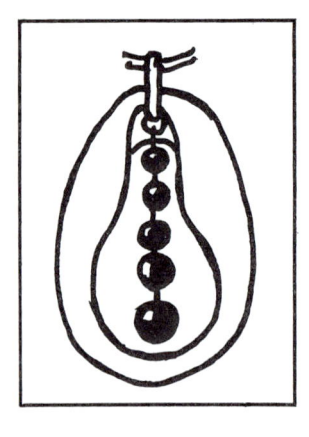

Fig. 2-5. Tin can opener pendant.

intervals. Tabs can be sprayed with acrylic clear. If you'd like more color, they can be painted with nail polish.

A bracelet can be made by using beer can openers and linking together as shown in Fig. 2-7.

WIRE AND BEAD RING

Buy about 5" of 16 gauge silver colored wire. Curl around a ¾" dowel stick, close together to make a circle. Measure around your finger with a strip of paper to get the size you will need to go over your knuckle. If the circle is too big, make them as small as you need them by pulling on the ends of wire. You want the wire to go around your finger twice with the two ends extending over about ¼". Curl these ends up slightly. Find two beads the same color about ¼" in diameter. Glue onto the ends of wire, but do not let the wire go all the way through, only about halfway. Allow glue to dry thoroughly. To hide the hole in the top of the bead, use a small

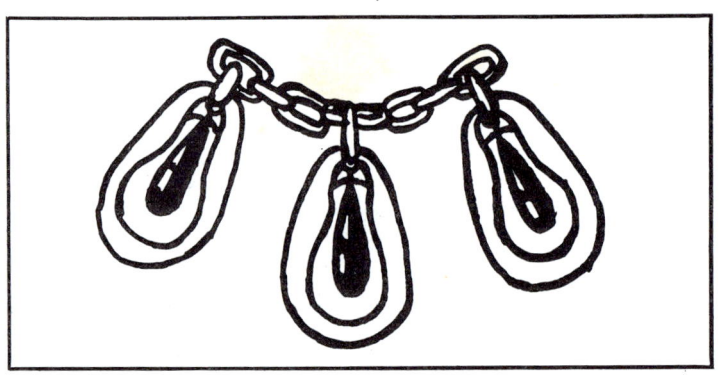

Fig. 2-6. Tin can opener necklace.

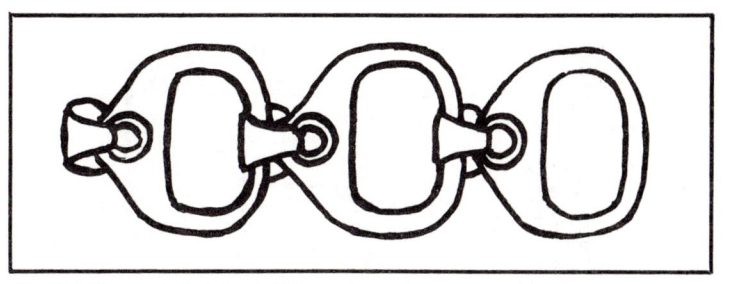

Fig. 2-7. Tin can opener bracelet.

headed pearl pin. Cut the pin off ⅛" from pearl. Glue it into the hole (Fig. 2-8).

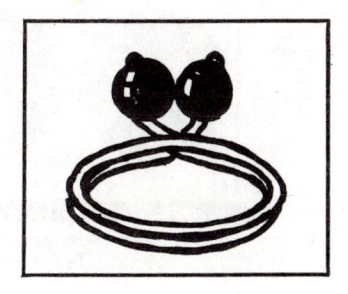

TIN CAN BRACELET

Use a tuna fish can or one of the same size. Cut off the top and bottom. File edges to make sure they are smooth, and then use emery paper for extra smoothness.

With tin shears, cut the can in half. Cut the extra tin off, round edges and smooth as before. Polish tin to as high a gloss as you can get. With enamel paints, paint designs in turquoise and black to represent an Indian bracelet. If you need to trace a design, use carbon paper. When the enamel is dry, shape the bracelet to fit the wrist by bending it around your wrist. Give the completed bracelet a coat of clear acrylic to keep its shine (Figs 2-9 and 2-10).

AZTEC SUN GOD PENDANT

Roll out self hardening clay on the wrong side of *linoleum* with a rolling pin until it is about 2½" square and ⅜" thick.

Trace a design onto thin paper and onto clay with an orange stick by pressing design lines. Cut around the outside edge and press the edge down so it bevels. A hole for hanging can be made by using a ball-point pen. While still a little damp, lines can be cleaned if ragged by wetting with a brush and water. Allow for thorough drying.

Fig. 2-8. Wire and bead ring.

Fig. 2-9. The tin can bracelet.

When dry, take a good brushful of orange enamel and drip it onto the clay. Do the same with yellow, allowing them to overlap in some places. Pick up the pendant and hold it by the edge, allowing colors to mingle and run together in some places. If done correctly, it will resemble *onyx*. Do not allow the paint to fill up lines. Insert a jump ring through the hole for hanging (Figs. 2-11 and 2-12).

HEART PIN

Take a piece of red felt and draw a heart. Take a piece of white felt and cut a smaller heart. Glue the white heart in the middle of the red heart, using fabric glue.

Take a small safety pin and fasten it with glue or sew it on the back of the red heart. You can decorate the white heart with *sequins* and seed beads with lace around the edges of the heart. Use glue for fastening (Fig. 2-13).

RUBBER CORD BRACELET

With a strip of paper, measure around the wrist to see how long you will need to make the bracelet. Lay the paper flat and mark

Fig. 2-10. You can use a tuna fish can to make the bracelet.

Fig. 2-11. Top view of the clay Aztec pendant.

it off, starting at one end with 1" and then ¼", 1" and ¼" until you reach the end of the paper. End up with ¼" even if it is a little longer than you need. This will tell you how many squares of wood you will need and how many beads, depending on their size. If you use ¼" beads, you will need about ten: if the beads are smaller, like ⅛", double the number.

Cut from ¼" hardboard as many 1" squares as you need. Smooth all edges.

Hold squares on a vise. With a ⅛" drill bit, drill two holes through each square as shown in Fig. 2-14. Paint with enamels or poster paint any color you wish. You may alternate colors or make them all the same. Paint both sides and all edges.

Now choose beads that are to go between the squares of any color that goes with the color of the blocks. If you are going to use ⅛" beads, four will go between each block, two at the top and two at the bottom. If you use ¼" beads, you will need only two between each block. Buy a spool of elastic cord-like thread. Starting at the square end push one piece through the top hole in the square, then through the bead, and then through another square until you come to the end. Leave about 1" over at each end. You can tie a temporary knot in the ends so that the cord will not slip out. Do the same with the holes at the bottom of the squares. When all are strung, tie the cords at the top together so there is no cord showing between

Fig. 2-12. Side view of the clay Aztec pendant.

Fig. 2-13. Heart pin.

squares and beads. Do not, however, stretch the cord. Do the same at the bottom. Push a knot inside of the hole in the square so nothing shows.

JEWELRY BOX FOR DAD

International coffee cans are just the thing for this project. Save the tab openers for jewelry.

Fig. 2-14. Rubber band bracelet.

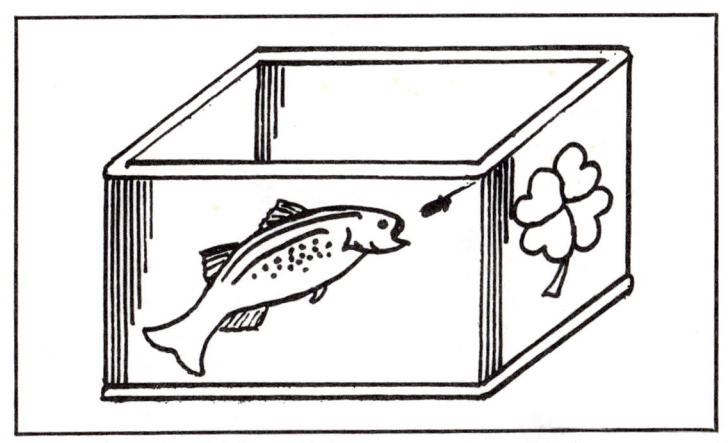

Fig. 2-15. Side view of the jewelry box.

Smooth the inside of the can with a file and then emery paper. Spray the can with whatever color you wish. Do not forget to cover the bottom and top rim. The top rim especially will need to be covered on the inside as well.

Line the bottom and sides of the inside can with velour paper, felt or soft material. Glue with a good white glue.

Find two pictures of Dad's favorite things, like sports (emblems or pictures of sports figures), hobbies or whatever he is particularly interested in. Horses, dogs and deer are good to use, too. Paste each on both of the long sides of the can.

Cut from paper or felt two four leaf clovers and glue them to the short sides. If you have used paper cutouts, spray the entire can with a clear acrylic. If you use felt cutouts, you'll have to spray the acrylic on before you glue them on.

Leave the lid clear, but with a permanent ink marking pen print the word "DAD" in the middle of the top (Figs. 2-15 and 2-16).

Fig. 2-16. Print the word "Dad" on the jewelry box.

Fig. 2-17. Star earrings.

STAR EARRINGS

Use the iridescent automotive foil you can get at auto supply stores that is adhesive backed. Trace design of a star onto a clear plastic lid and cut it out. Adhere a piece of foil to one side that is a little bigger than a star. Cut around the star.

Do the same to the other side. Pierce a hole where indicated with a hot needle. Insert a jump ring. Attach another jump ring to that, and use the earring back for the drop pendant attachment to the earring (Fig. 2-17).

LEATHER PENDANT

Trace the pattern of the design outline onto medium weight leather of a neutral color. Trace each of the other two parts of the

Fig. 2-18. Leather pendant.

design that are on top of the outline onto a little lighter weight leather of the same color. Cut each one separately. Punch holes in the top of the base design and fringe the bottom.

Color each of the other two pieces a different color with leather dyes. When dry, cement on top of the base as shown (Fig. 2-18). Polish.

CLAY MOUSE PIN

Use self hardening clay and roll out a piece about 1" long and ½" high at back. Shape according to the pattern and smooth.

While still damp, use a needle to make three holes for the mouse's whiskers on each side of the front. Use a pencil point or ball-point pen to make holes for the eyes and slots for the ears and tail. When dry, paint with enamels. The mouse can be painted gray with tan and with a white nose, or paint it all white.

For a white mouse, use pink Indian beads for eyes. For a tan and gray mouse, use black. Cut from this leather or plastic ears to insert in slots. Use tan for a tan mouse, gray for a gray mouse and white for a white mouse. For the white mouse, ears may be painted pink on the inside, and the tan mouse's ears can be white on the inside.

Cut 3 inches length of a corresponding color ⅛" gimp for the tail and insert. Glue the pin back to the mouse (Fig. 2-19).

GRAPE PIN

Roll out self hardening clay on the back side of oil cloth with a rolling pin to about ⅛" thickness. Trace pattern number 1 on paper, cut out, lay on clay and cut around it. Do not let it dry out.

Roll grapes with your fingers (about 20 or so). Attach to leaves, placing some on top of others.

Draw veins in leaves with a pencil for realism. Give the leaves some shape by bending the ends down or up or to one side.

When thorougly dry, paint grapes a blue violet and leaves green. As with all self hardening clay, you may paint with enamel, or use liquitex or poster paint and spray with a clear acrylic for

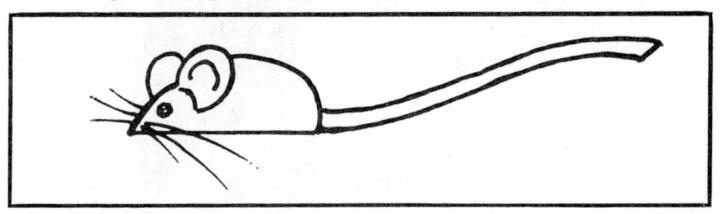

Fig. 2-19. Clay mouse pin.

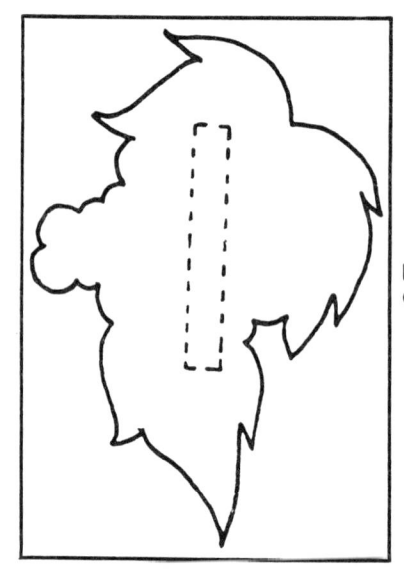

Fig. 2-20. View of the base for the clay grape pin.

gloss. Glue the pin back to back on dotted lines (Fig. 2-20 and 2-21).

SLATE PIN

Take an old piece of slate. Use a hacksaw or sawtooth knife and cut the pin to the size you wish, such as 2″ long and 1″ wide.

Fig. 2-21. View of the grapes in place.

Fig. 2-22. Slate pin.

Because of the difficulty in cutting slate, use pieces that have been broken off of an old roof or found at a slate quarry.

Glue the pin on back of the piece of slate. Decorate the front piece of slate by painting a flower in yellow with a green stem (Fig. 2-22).

LENS PENDANT

If you can get lenses that are not bifocals, this is best; however, if the line does not show up too prominently, you must use them. Clean the glass well first.

There are some tiny dried flowers that you can use to make a design in the center of the lens, or day parts of weeds yourself and color them. Arrange them in the center of the glass with a fair sized amount of space around them.

Fig. 2-23. Lens pendant.

97

Fig. 2-24. An attractive modern clay pendant.

You may wish to use a tiny butterfly or picture from a magazine. Whatever you choose, use a paste or glue that will dry clear so that it doesn't show. Glue the design on. Paste a background of paper, a color that will show off the design. You can use a tiny border of lace first if you wish.

Use a gold or silver braid glued to the outside rim of the glass as a border. Leave a small loop at the top for a jump ring (Fig. 2-23).

Fig. 2-25. The owl felt pin.

MODERN CLAY PENDANT

Use self hardening clay. Roll out as for the grape pin, but slightly thinner, and cut out. Allow it to dry. Trace the design onto clay by rubbing the back of the design with soft pencil. Before it is thoroughly dry, put a hole in the top for hanging.

This pendant is more attractive if colored with a flat light paint for the background. Wall paint may be used. Color half moons with gold paint, stars with silver. Lines may be made with permanent black marking pens (Fig. 2-24).

OWL FELT PIN

Cut out pieces of brown felt in the shape of an owl that you have traced from a bird book onto paper. Sew on the back of the owl a tiny gold safety pin for fastening.

Use a black magic marker and decorate the face with eyes, nose and mouth. You can stitch pieces of felt for the face. Use black felt for the eyes and nose and gold for the eyes. Movable eyes are always fun to use (Fig. 2-25).

ARROW HEAD NECKLACE

Take an arrow head and wind silver wire around the two upper points (let an extra piece of wire be made into a loop and twisted with pliers) and then down the back to catch the point. With a small pair of pliers, turn the ends of silver wire tight.

Through the loop at the top, attach a chain. Wear this artifact safely around your neck (Fig. 2-26).

Fig. 2-26. Arrow head necklace.

Fig. 2-27. Snowflake glass.

OLD SNOWFLAKE GLASS

You may be fortunate to have old antique snowflake glass from a church or community building. Use your glass cutter to cut out the design. Then apply lead around the edges to protect the glass, leaving a loop open at the top for hanging. These treasures are hung with fish line so they look as if they are floating in the air (Fig. 2-27).

TIEPIN

There may be an old tiepin around the house that nobody wears anymore. If so, you can use this as long as it has a base on which you can glue something. If not tiepins can be purchased fairly cheap from a craft shop.

From clay, form a *scarab* beetle about ½" long, ¼" wide and ¼"high, like half an egg. Using a pencil, mark off on the top shape of the scarab for the legs, two reaching above the bug's head and two

Fig. 2-28. Scarab beetle tiepin.

reaching in back. Color the scarab with bright colored enamels. Glue to the backing of the pin. If the pin does not have a flat disc on which to glue the scarab, before painting push the pin into the scarab in back. Glue onto the pin when the scarab is finished (Fig. 2-28).

FEATHER STATIONERY

Draw the design of the swan neck, the lines of the water and the grasses and cattails very lightly on your paper first. If you think you can paint the swan's neck, head and beak without having to draw it first, you can eliminate the drawing. Make sure they are placed in the proper place so that when you add the feather, it does not cover the design.

There are black swans as well as white, so choose the color of your stationery accordingly. A darker color stationery can be used if you make your swan white.

Paint the head and neck. Add the beak, grasses, cattails and water lines. When they are dry, paste your feather on top for the body. (Fig. 2-29).

CLOVE APPLE

Use a good winter-keeping apple like a Staymen, Winesap or MacIntosh. Stick whole cloves in the apple as close as possible until the whole apple is covered.

Try to finish the apple all at one time. It will hurt your fingers, so take small rest periods.

Fig. 2-29. Feather stationery.

Fig. 2-30. Clove apple.

Tie a red ribbon onto the stem. If there is no stem, stick a toothpick into the stem area, wind with ribbon and make a bow.

Allow the apple to dry completely for at least one week. This apple will last for years. The cloves preserve it, and it will become very light in weight. The apple is fine for bureau drawers and for hanging. An orange or lemon may be used instead of the apple if you wish (Fig. 2-30).

LEATHER AND FOIL BARRETTE

You can obtain a piece of sole leather from most shoe companies for nothing. Trace the pattern of the barrette onto the leather and cut out with a sharp knife. Make the holes with a leather punch or ice pick.

Buy a piece of adhesive backed iridescent foil from automotive stores. It is usually sold to use on cars as a decorative piece. Peel off the back and adhere to the barrette. Cut the holes and the center out as before.

Use a meat skewer for the part that goes through the barrette. Cut it the size you need and spray paint silver (Fig. 2-31).

GLASSES CASE

Trace the pattern onto felt of a desired color and cut out. Sew the braid on where indicated. Sew the sides of case together up to point marked on pattern. Cutouts of colored felt may be glued or sewed on, adding beads or sequins for the center of the flower (Fig. 2-32).

COMB CASE

Use a heavy felt or upholstery material. Lay a small comb on the piece of material and outline with a pencil the size of the comb, leaving ½" more for sewing. You may find it easier to first draw a pattern on a piece of paper and then onto the material.

Cut the material to fit and sew with a heavy thread, knotting both ends well. Cut a slight curve at the top as an opening for easy access for the comb. Decorate the comb case with initials or designs of colored felt on the front of the case (Fig. 2-33).

TINY CUSHION SCENTS

Cut scraps of gay colored material 2" to 3" square. Sew up three sides.

Use dry herbs and stuff a tiny fabric cushion. Sew the fourth side closed with small stitches.

You can decorate cushions by sewing lace around the outside. If the fabric is plain, you can embroider with thread or yarn.

These sweet cushions make nice bureau drawer or linen closet scents. Other scents that can be used are dry rose petals, dried geranium leaves, shredded pine needles and kitchen spices (Fig. 2-34).

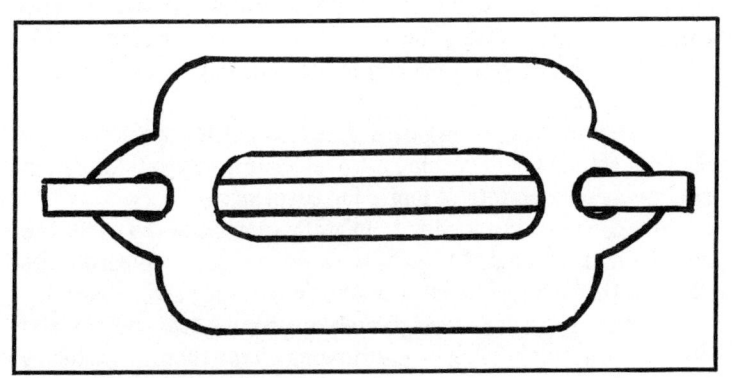

Fig. 2-31. Leather and foil barrette.

Fig. 2-32. Felt glasses case.

DOLLHOUSE

Select a nice sized grocery carton. Cut out the front panel, and lay out the rooms you would like in your own house.

Cut out cardboard and make partitions between rooms. Use bright colored rickrack over the ends of the cardboard so the house is attractive. Cut openings for doorways and windows on outside walls. Use bits of fabric to decorate the house by cutting curtains and making rugs.

Make furniture of cardboard. Use tiny bottle caps and empty spools of thread for furnishings. Cover chairs with bits of cotton and glue or sew on bits of fabric for coverings.

You can use old samples from wallpaper books to paper the walls. Paint the ceilings and woodwork. Make your people from bits of clay and dress them in leftover scraps from the sewing basket.

Another easy dollhouse to create is to use two shelves of a bookcase in a child's room by partitioning off the rooms with heavy cardboard cut and taped to the top of the inside of the book shelf.

Fig. 2-33. Felt comb case.

When the child tires of the house, clean it off and replace the books (Fig. 2-35).

WASTEBASKET

At a grocery or ice cream store, find an empty bulk ice cream carton. Paint it with a solid color enamel base. When dry, decorate it with cutouts from magazines or seals from a stationery store. Around the top and bottom edges, glue rickrack or ornamental cording. Spar varnish to preserve (Fig. 2-36).

Fig. 2-34. Tiny cushion scents.

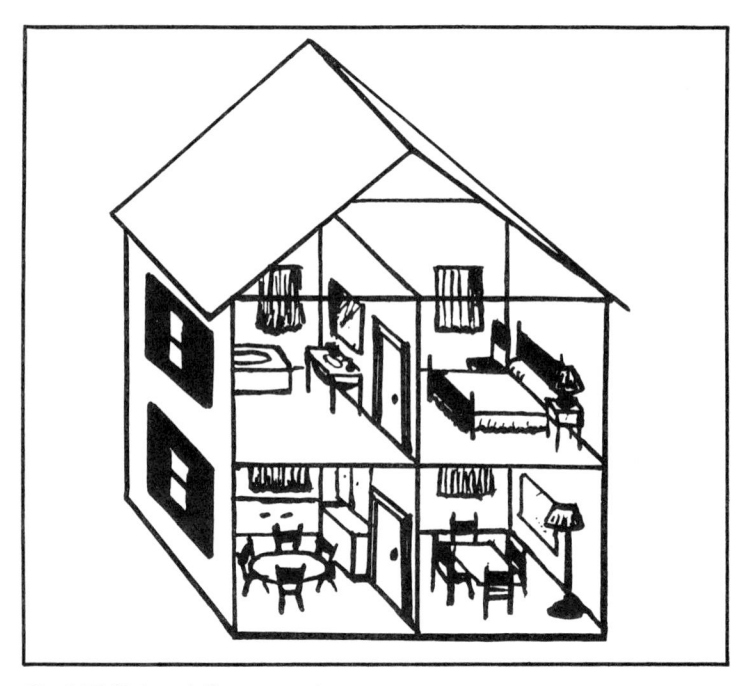

Fig. 2-35. Make a dollhouse out of a grocery carton.

YARN HOLDER

Use an empty milk carton. Glue some leftover contact paper around the box. Cut a round hole about ⅛" in the center of the lid, and one on either side of the box near the top of the box.

Fig. 2-36. A bulk ice cream carton makes a nice wastebasket.

Fig. 2-37. Use an empty milk carton for the yarn holder.

Use reinforcements over the holes to strengthen them. Glue a wide ribbon around the edge of the cover.

Take another piece of ribbon about 3½" wide, putting the ends of the ribbon through the holes on the side of the box. Tie a knot on each end inside the box. Place a ball of yarn inside the box. Pull the yarn through the hole in the top cover, placing the top on the box securely (Fig. 2-37).

Fig. 2-38. Top view of the desk blotter.

107

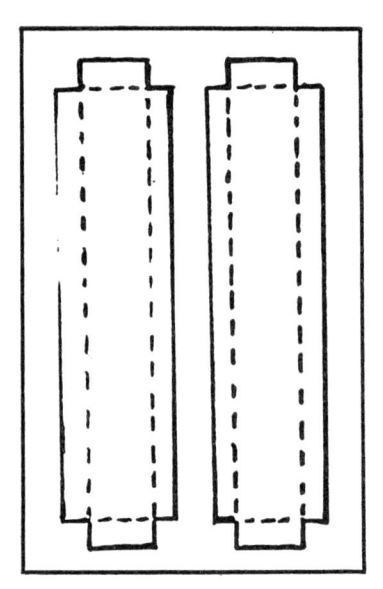

Fig. 2-39. Construction detail for the desk blotter.

DESK BLOTTER

Use heavy cardboard that is about ½" longer than your blotter but the same size from top to bottom. Cut two pieces of lighter weight cardboard for the sides—the same height as the blotter but 2½" wide.

Fig. 2-40. The butterfly bobby pin.

108

Contact paper works very well for this project and will hold tightly. Cut two strips of contact paper for side pieces 1" bigger on all four sides. Cut out corners as indicated. Paste one long edge on the strip of cardboard. Lay the cardboard strip on top of the edge of large cardboard and fold the extra piece to the back at the sides and top. Do the same with the other piece.

Cover the entire back of cardboard with the same contact paper. Slip the blotter into open sides (Figs. 2-38 and 2-39).

BUTTERFLY BOBBY PIN

Trace the pattern onto acetate as for the mobile and color with marking pens on both sides. Use a thin black pipe cleaner for the body and nylon bristles for the antenna. Follow the same procedure as for the mobile. Sew by punching the needle through acetate and around the body, on the top wire of the bobby pin (Fig. 2-40).

FLOWER BASKET

Take a small plastic berry box and lace red velvet ribbon through the holes. Finish with a bow at the top of the basket.

Tie a piece of velvet at one end of the top of the basket. Make a loop for a handle, fastening at the other end of the other side.

Fill the basket with fall plastic flowers. Use it as a May basket or fill it with artificial small fruits (Fig. 2-41).

FOAM BALL PIN CUSHION

Cut a 3" styrofoam ball in half. Drape a piece of soft jersey material over the ball, and pin it to the ball all around as evenly as

Fig. 2-41. Plastic flower basket.

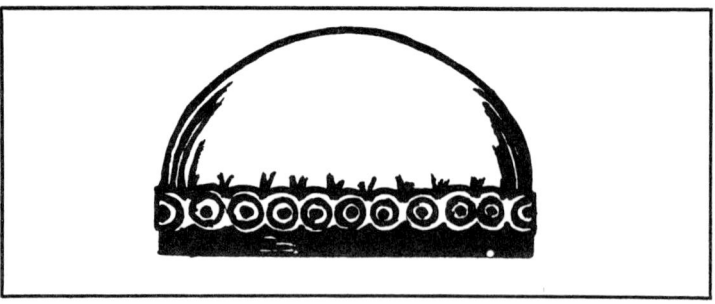

Fig. 2-42. Foam ball pin cushion.

possible. Cut off what jersey hangs below the base of the ball. Remove pins and try to put the flat bottom of the ball into half of a plastic typewriter ribbon container. If it is a little too big, press with your fingers all around the edge. It will compress about ¼" up from the bottom. Press until it will fit into the can.

Gather thread around the edge of the jersey about ⅛" in with very small stitches, and tie around the base of the ball. Spread the gathers as evenly as possible and glue the covering to the ball. Most of these tins are red. If you wish to change the color, spray paint gold or silver. When dry, glue the covered half ball to the bottom of the can, pressing it in firmly. Use ½" braid to cover where the can and material touch (fig. 2-42).

BOOKWORM BOOKENDS

Enlarge the pattern, trace and cut from ½" wood or press board. Smooth edges with sandpaper.

Enlarge the pattern of the worm and trace onto 1" thick wood. Cut out and glue the front to one side of the bookend and the rest to the other side.

Paint the background green to represent grass. Paint the worm orange with black stripes.

Fig. 2-43. Pattern for the back piece of the bookworm bookend.

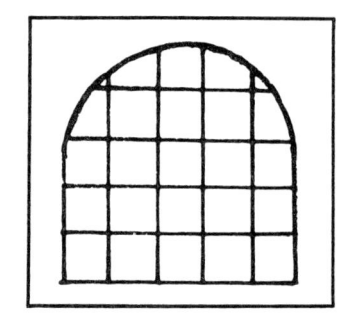

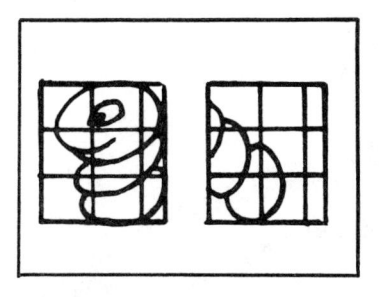

Fig. 2-44. Pattern for the worm for the bookend.

Fig. 2-45. Assembly of the front piece of the bookend.

Drill ¼" holes on each side of the head and insert 2" of black pipe cleaners. Add movable eyes to each side and paint a smiling mouth. Add 3" × 5" piece of metal beneath the bottom at the rear to put under books (Figs. 2-43 through 2-46).

PENCIL HOLDER

Use a can about the size of a Campbell's soup can. Cut off the top and smooth the edge. You can cover the can with felt or velour paper in white.

Draw two clubs (copy from cards) from black felt, two spades from black felt, and two diamonds and two hearts from red. You do not have to use felt. If you like, you can use metal paper or just plain construction paper. Cut them out and glue to the outside of the can illustrated (Fig. 2-47). Glue some gold braid around the top and bottom of the can.

Your pencil holder can be made to match the desk blotter if you wish by covering the can with the same contact paper you used for the desk blotter. This way you will have a set.

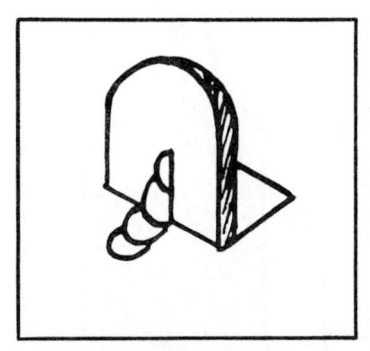

Fig. 2-46. Assembly of the back piece of the bookend.

Fig. 2-47. Pencil holder.

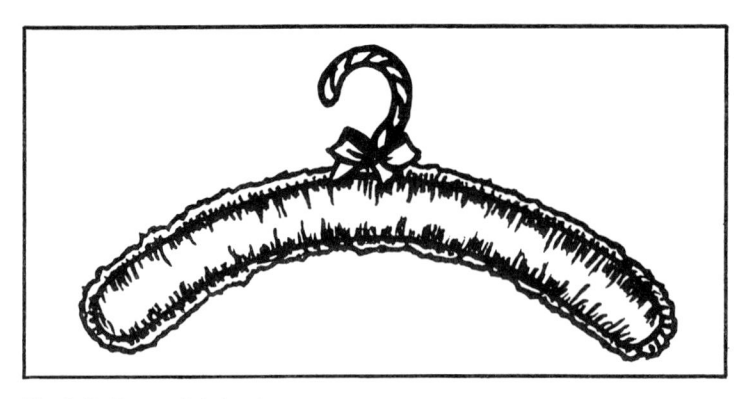

Fig. 2-48. Covered clothes hanger.

COVERED HANGERS

Buy some wooden dress hangers in a quarter dollar store. Cut a rectangular piece of fabric from the scrap basket—a little larger than your hanger.

Cover the wooden hanger completely with 1" of cotton quilt batting or wind hanger with old silk stockings. Take the rectangular piece of fabric and pin it tightly around the hanger until it takes the shape of the hanger.

Sew the pinned edges with small stitches. If you wish, put some sachet or sweet smelling herbs inside of the cover. Wrap around hanger hook ribbon and fasten with a few stitches. Make a pretty bow in the front with leftover ribbon and sew fast to the hanger (Fig. 2-48).

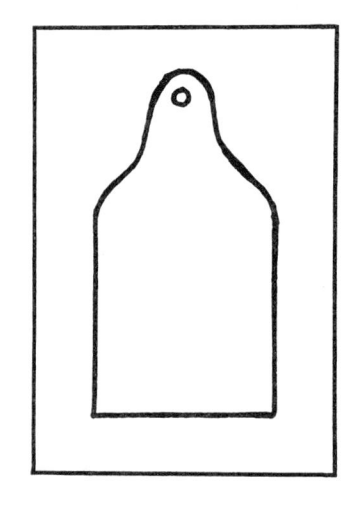

Fig. 2-49. Cheese cutting board background.

Fig. 2-50. Cheese cutting board showing placement of tile.

CHEESE CUTTING BOARD

Use a very hard wood for this such as maple, oak, apple or ash about ¾" thick and about 15" or 16" long. Enlarge the fish pattern, trace onto wood and cut out. Sand all edges smooth. Drill the hole for the fish's eye. It will also do to hang the board up (Figs. 2-49 and 2-50).

Fig. 2-51. The snow jar makes a nice paperweight.

Fig. 2-52. Mason jar garden.

SNOW JAR

Use an empty baby food jar. Scrub it well and dry.

Place a piece of clay in the bottom of the jar. Make a winter picture scene by using artificial trees, miniature deer and small red holly berries. Insert the material into the clay. Be sure to use a waterproof glue. Let the clay dry thoroughly.

Fill the jar with water almost to the top. Add one scant teaspoon of artificial snow. Screw the lid on tightly.

Shake up the jar and you will see snowflakes. It makes a nice paperweight for the desk or a nice gift for a shut-in (Fig. 2-51).

MASON JAR GARDENS

Select a pretty quart jar and fill it about 3" with kitty litter or sand. Sink artificial foilage and flowers or dried weeds and flowers in the litter or sand.

Screw a zinc cap on top of the jar. This makes a nice hospital gift with no maintenance (Fig. 2-52).

COCKTAIL APRON

The cocktail apron is made of black material, either felt or linen. Cut a square of any shape you wish; a good size is 11" x 11".

If felt is used, there is no need to sew. Merely pink the edges. If other material is used, it will be necessary to hem the sides and bottom of the apron first. Leave the top unfinished until painting or application of the design is complete. The design may be cut from colored felt and glued on with glue that is dry cleanable. If you wish to paint the design on, the entire design must be painted white with a fabric paint first. On each part of the design the color it should be is marked by initials: W-white, O-orange, Y-yellow, R-red, T-turquoise, G-green, and the center of the eye is black. When the design is complete, add a gold sequin.

Cut two pieces of 1" black grosgrain long enough to tie in back. Cut an extra piece of material or felt for the top. Sew this onto the top of the apron as a band, inserting the ribbon as shown in Figs. 2-53 and 2-54).

BARBECUE APRON

Enlarge the pattern and trace on paper. Pin to natural colored butcher linen or canvas and cut out. Cut from the same material a piece 1" wider than the width of the apron and about 6" wide. Use wide red bias tape for around the apron. Sew a piece of the bias tape

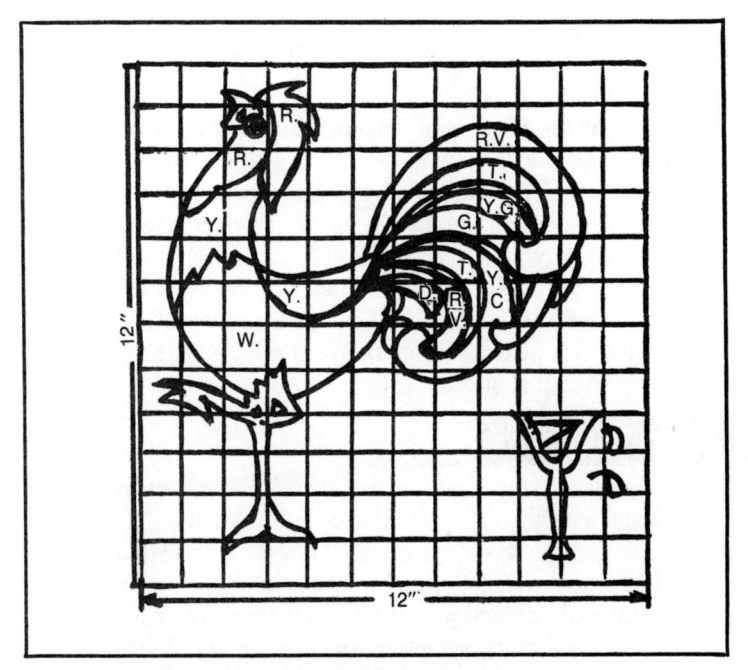

Fig. 2-53. Pattern for the rooster and glass for the cocktail apron.

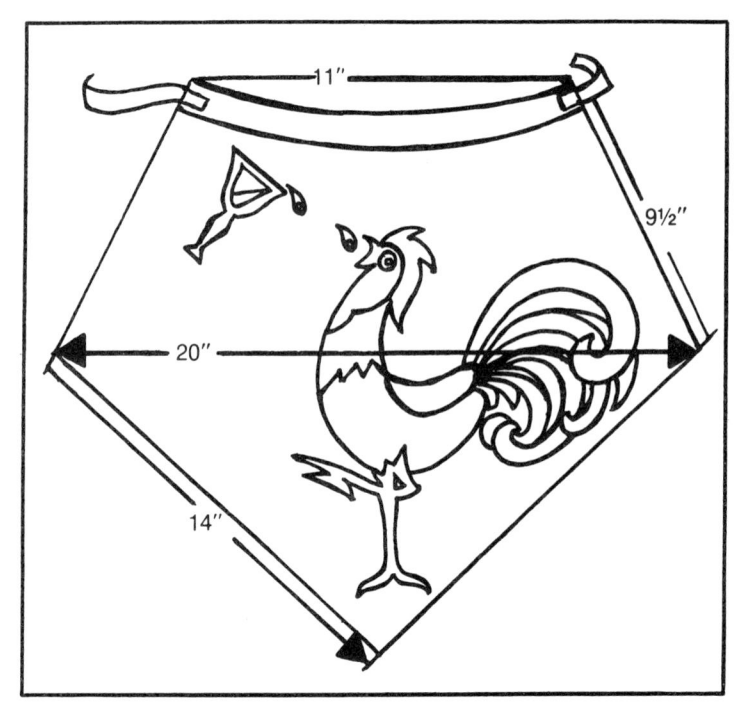

Fig. 2-54. Placement of the rooster and glass for the apron. Note the size of the apron.

to one side of the extra piece of material. Pin this onto the bottom of the apron for pockets, with tape at the top. Sew on a sewing machine around the sides and through the middle to form two pockets. Sew bias tape around the entire apron. Sew the red ribbon at the side for tying around the waist.

Trace the pattern of hamburger bun onto tan felt and the hamburger onto brown felt. Use light green felt for lettuce or lace if you prefer; sew beneath hamburger gathering a little and sew one side only so that it sticks out (Fig. 2-55).

STENCILED SCARF

Use a plastic lid. Trace the design on it and cut out. With fabric colors and a very stiff brush, take up a little paint.

Brush it on a paper first so that it is almost dry. When applied, it will be streaky. Start at the point of the milkweed and stroke toward the end, through stencil. The milkweed does not have to be white; lavender makes an interesting flower, too. When dry, the seed may be painted brown (Fig. 2-56).

CORSAGE HOLDER

Ask your doctor to save you a small vial about 2" or 3" long and ½" wide. Clean it out well. You can use thin floral wire for the holder. Glue around the top of the vial about three or four rings. When wrapping around the vial, insert a large corsage pin under the wire with the top just above the top of the vial. Now you can put water in the vial and keep your corsage or flower longer (Fig. 2-57).

WATERING CAN FUN

Purchase a child's watering can and decorate it with glued on pieces of felt with borders of tiny artificial flowers. Patchwork squares of material outlined with rickrack or braid make a quaint can. This makes a nice Mother's Day gift and a centerpiece for a party (Fig. 2-58).

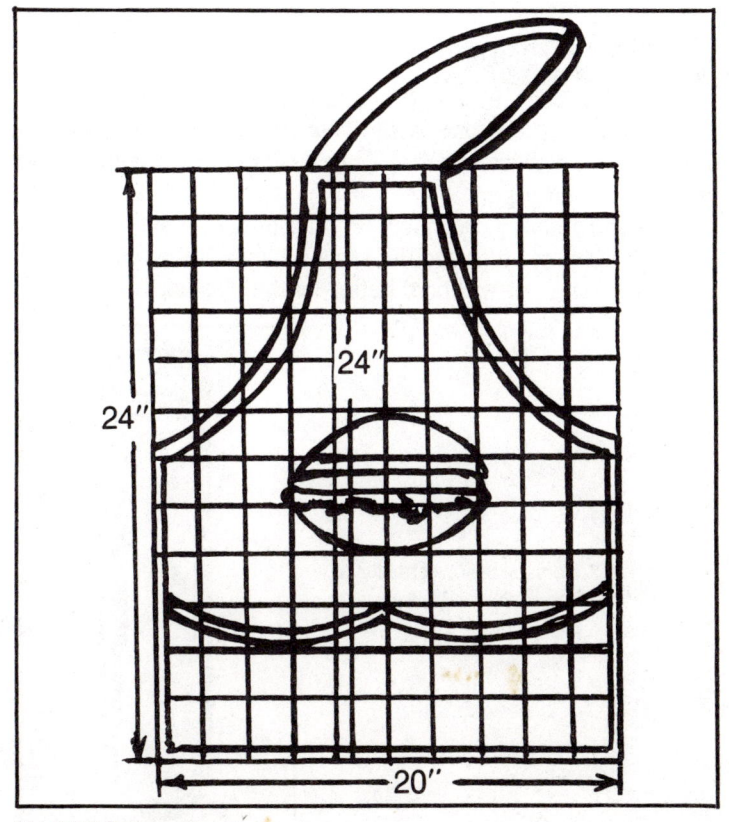

Fig. 2-55. Barbecue apron.

Fig. 2-56. Stenciled scarf.

EMBOSSED SILVER BOX

General Foods International coffee cans are a good size for the box, or buy a wooden one to suit your taste. Spray paint the can inside and out with white paint. Trace designs onto the sides of the box with carbon paper.

Glue an ordinary cord about ⅛" thick over the lines of the box. Use white glue for this. Do the same thing with the top, but use rubber cement as it will hold better on the plastic.

Fig. 2-57. Corsage or flower holder.

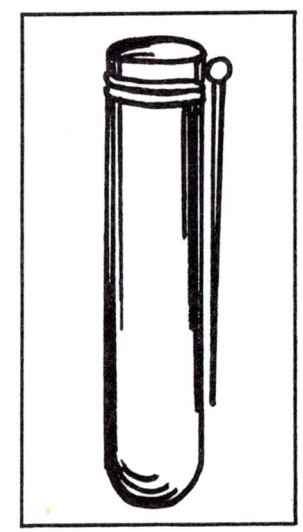

Fig. 2-58. This watering can is decorated with artificial flowers.

When dry, crumple a piece of silver foil (Reynolds wrap) that is larger than the box. This will give the covering an antique look. Uncrumple and carefully cover the raised design, pushing it down around edges with an orange stick. Be careful not to tear the paper. Use rubber cement. Do not cover the top edge or it will interfere with the top when placed on the box. If you do not like the white paint showing, this edge may be painted silver. Do the same with the top of the box as you did the sides, but cover to the edge and not under.

Using black liquitex or acrylic paint, cover over the entire design. When dry, wipe off all paint except around edges and in cracks. You will find it will give a very nice antique effect to your box (Figs. 2-59 through 2-61).

LETTER OPENER

You can use heavy tin can metal for the blade of the opener or get a piece of 4" × 1" 18 gauge brass. Enlarge the pattern of the

Fig. 2-59. Side view of the silver box.

Fig. 2-60. End view of the silver box.

blade, trace on metal and cut out. If you use brass, you will need a jewelry saw frame and blade to cut it. The tin can be cut with tin shears. File the edges by beveling so that they become smooth and sharp enough to open an envelope.

Cut a piece of any type of wood, 4" long × 1" × ½". In one end, saw a slit wide enough for the metal to slip into and across the middle as shown in Fig. 2-62. File the edges of the wood so that they are slightly rounded, including the back end.

Smooth the metal with emery paper and polish. Stain the handle or paint it with enamel. Glue the blade into the slot.

HAND PRINT

Mix up a batch of plaster of paris in a small bowl. Mold into a round shape as big as your hand and spread out about 1" thick.

Place the palm of your hand in the middle of the plaster. Embed it so you can see your hand print.

Fig. 2-61. Top view of the silver box.

Let the cast dry partially. Before completely dry, turn around carefully and press a hairpin or paper clip for hanging into the plaster.

The following day take a bright royal blue enamel and paint the finger prints. Children love to give this gift to their grandparents (Figs. 2-63 and 2-64).

WOODEN HANGERS

Purchase some wooden dress and pants hangers. Paint them with a solid coat of enamel paint.

Decorate them with your own paintings, monograms or use cutouts from flower magazines or seals from a stationery store. Give them a coat of spar varnish to seal pores (Fig. 2-65).

EASEL PICTURE

Cut four pieces of dowel stick ½" thick. Three pieces must be 6" long and the third 4" long. With a sharp knife, shave two sides of

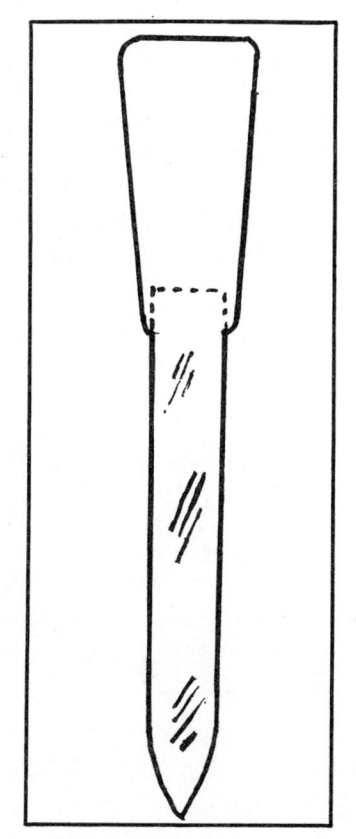

Fig. 2-62. Letter opener.

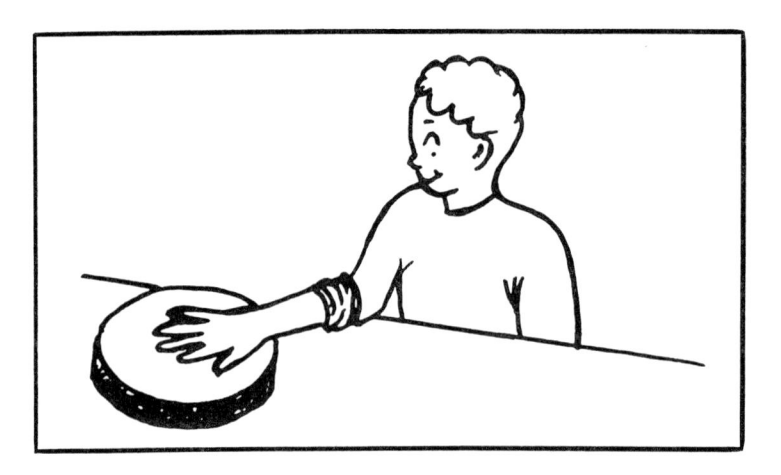

Fig. 2-63. To make the print, the palm of the hand is placed in the plaster.

one stick thin. Make sure they are opposite to each other. Start about ½" from top and shave until the end is about 1/16" thick. The front and back of the dowel will still be round. On the other two long sticks, do the same but only on one side of the end.

About ⅜" from the top of the shaved ends, drill holes through all three. Make sure they are in the same place. You will need a very small drill bit. Use a *cotter pin* small enough to go through holes and long enough to stick out about ⅛" after going through all three pieces. Bend them flat against the dowel. This forms your

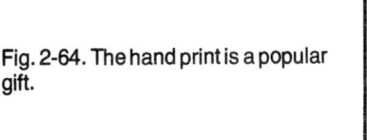

Fig. 2-64. The hand print is a popular gift.

Fig. 2-65. Painted wooden hanger.

easel. Lay the third dowel across the front of the easel about 2" from the bottom. Mark with pencil a dot in the center of the small dowel about ½" from each end. Mark on each front leg a dot 2" from bottom. Drill small holes in all marked places. That will be four holes. Insert a small brad into the hole of the cross piece and into the leg. Bend over in the back.

Cut a piece of 3/16" hardboard 4" × 3". This will be the backing for your picture. It's easy to find a picture that will fit that

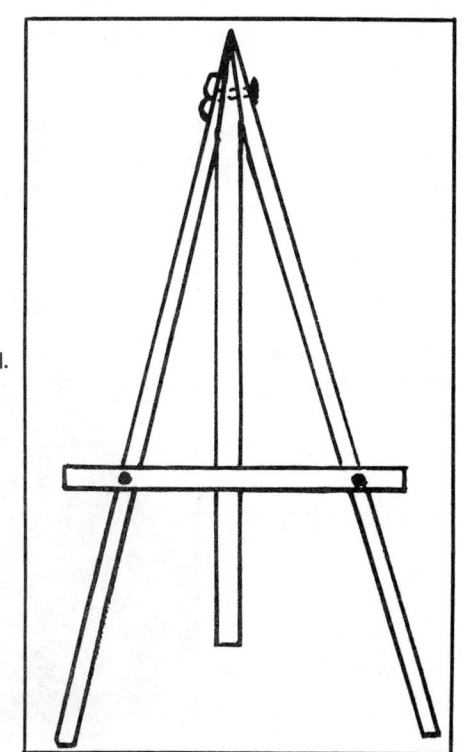

Fig. 2-66. The finished easel.

Fig. 2-67. Spice rope.

size if you make a *template*. Cut a piece of thin cardboard or paper about 5 × 4. Cut out the center 3" × 4". Use this to lay over magazine pictures you find until you get one that suits and fits the opening. Cut out, glue on hardboard and give a couple coats of clear

Fig. 2-68. Put some plants in the terrarium.

Fig. 2-69. Straw wreath.

acrylic spray. Spray paint your easel with gold and place your picture on the stand (Fig. 2-66).

SPICE ROPE

During the summer gather different types of herbs and dry them. If you wish to make this craft during the winter, you can purchase herbs and spices in bulk.

Braid twine or colored pieces of fabric into a rope 2' long. Cut square pieces of fabric 4" × 4" and lay them out on a table.

In the center of each square, place a tablespoon of spice or herb powder or leaves. Gather up ends and tie tightly at the top of the square. Hang them at intervals on braided rope and tie tightly

Fig. 2-70. Create a desert with different varieties of cactus.

125

Fig. 2-71. Fancy jelly glass covers.

with a cord. They make great gifts and are used in kitchens and linen closets for good smelling (Fig. 2-67).

TERRARIUMS

Select an empty clear glass bottle or jar. Wash it until it shines.

Take a trip to the woodland and gather in a basket some tiny ferns, moss, partridge berry, *pipsissewa*, acorns, tiny pine cones and some black earth from the forest floor.

Fig. 2-72. An example of a pine needle cat shape.

Do not cap the bottle. Plants need oxygen. Water when dry with a clothes sprinkler. Place the bottle in a shady window; remember the plants are from the woodland (Fig. 2-68).

STRAW WREATHS

In a florist's shop you can buy wreath forms. For the straw wreaths, group bunches of straw along the wreath and tie tightly with a strong cord to the wreath base. Be sure to make the wreath full and cover up the place where you tied cord. When the wreath is completed with the straw, start to decorate it. For example, wind a wide gold ribbon around the wreath. At intervals between the ribbon, insert some clusters of small pine cones wired to a short pick. You can use this basic straw wreath and change it at the different seasons of the year (Fig. 2-69).

SALAD BOWL GARDENING

Take a brown salad bowl and create a desert scene using different varieties of cactus. If the bowl is wooden, use heavy aluminum foil on the bottom. Then fill the bowl with an inch of small pebbles or gravel for drainage and a sandy mixture up to the top.

Plant the cactus. You may have to use a glove because some of the plants have long thorns. The *bunny ear cactus* has small thorns that feel soft, but when they get into your skin they irritate.

Fig. 2-73. Merry-go-round mobile.

Fig. 2-74. Water garden.

Add small attractive rocks to your garden and maybe a ceramic figure. Be sure to place the desert garden in the sunshine. And water when needed, usually once a week. Remember that these are desert plants and thrive on dry conditions (Fig. 2-70).

CARDBOARD DOLLS

Get some cardboard from a nearby store and lay it out on a table. Cut out pictures of men and women and children's figures from a magazine or catalog.

Paste pictures onto the cardboard and cut around the figures. If you wish them to stand, paste a small 1″ × 1″ piece of cardboard in back of the figures. Children enjoy playing with these paper dolls and often use them in their dollhouses.

FANCY JELLY COVERS

During jelly making time after jars have been filled and paraffin added, make the jars look like a gift. With your pinking shears, cut squares about 2 × 2 (according to your jar size). Cover the paraffin or the jar top and secure with a rubber band (Fig. 2-71).

PINE NEEDLE ART—PINE NEEDLE SHAPES

Gather pine needles under an evergreen tree. Find some scrap material in the work basket and cut a pattern of a flower, cat or dog or square 12 × 12. On the wrong side, sew up three sides, leaving one side open. Turn inside out and fill with pine needles until the shape is full. Sew neatly the remaining side.

Years ago these little pine needle shapes were popularly done in *calico* and old fashioned prints. Now one sees them in gift shops selling at a high price (Fig. 2-72).

MERRY-GO-ROUND MOBILE

Take some cardboard and place a saucer on it. Draw around the saucer and cut out. Paint cardboard a bright color.

With an ice pick, punch a small hole in the center. Knot a piece of heavy string and pull it through the cardboard. Punch some more holes around the circumference of the circle and leave different lengths of string knotted and hanging down from the cardboard.

Draw horses in different poses by tracing them from books and onto the cardboard. Cut them out and paint them on either side according to your taste.

Tie a horse to each string after you have punched through the body of the horse. Be sure to knot the string. Make sure the horses do not touch each other. Use different sized horses to balance the mobile.

If you wish to make the merry-go-round longer, you can add more strings and horses by knotting them securely to each other. Hang the mobile in a breezy place and watch the horses prance (Fig. 2-73).

WATER GARDEN

Take a shallow dish like a dish garden or centerpiece container. Fill it with water and clip small pieces of ivy or *philodendron* from a plant. Anchor it in the dish with pretty colored pebbles.

Fig. 2-75. Macaroni necklace.

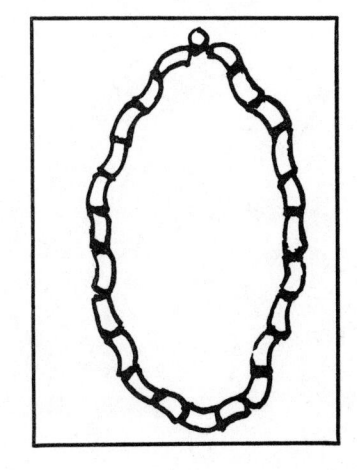

This water garden will grow and thrive as long as you keep the container filled with water. The vines will grow and will need to be clipped. Roots will grow because of the moisture. You can float candles among the vines for party time and add a ceramic figure (Fig. 2-74).

MACARONI BEADS

Lay out macaroni on a table. Tint the macaroni any color you wish, using food coloring or different colored enamel paints you have around the house.

String the macaroni with heavy nylon thread or lightweight nylon cord, using an embroidery needle. When the strand is long enough, knot the ends of the string with a small wooden bead. This will hold the macaroni in place and enable you to tie the ends together for fastening (Fig. 2-75).

Chapter 3
Brighten Up
The Holidays

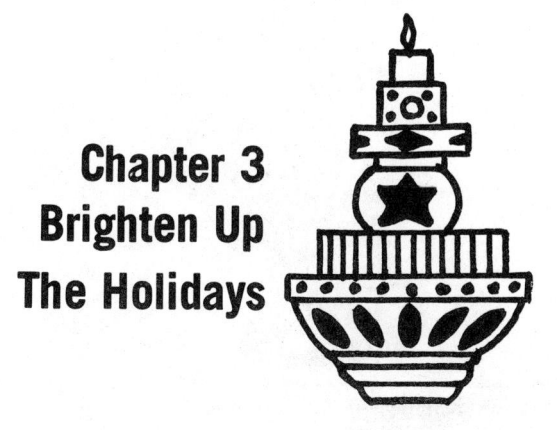

Holidays are festive occasions, times for families to get together and have fun, and everyone enjoys dressing up for them. So why not dress up your home, too? With a little extra effort on your part, you will be accepting compliments from all who come to visit.

Many of the decorations in this chapter are designed for a particular occasion, but with a little imagination and some slight modification they can be made to fit any holiday. Experiment with those in the book, but make sure you enjoy them as well for nothing can spoil a party quicker than a tired or bored hostess (Fig. 3-1).

CHRISTMAS DOOR DECORATION

You will need a reed woven circle about 18" in diameter. Hunt up some pine cones: seven about 4" × 2¼" that are fairly open, 10 pine cones 6" × 2" fairly closed. Collect some real or artificial Christmas greens such as mistletoe and holly, five red satin Christmas balls, five green ones, five silver balls about ½" in diameter, silver glitter, snowflake glitter, fine floral wire, white waterproof paint and a good white glue.

On the red balls, paint with glue a five petaled flower about 2" in diameter and sprinkle with silver glitter. Put a piece of floral wire through the holes of your silver balls and through the center of the red ball. Make the wire long enough to be able to go through the spaces in the woven circle and twist in back to hold them on. Leave the green balls plain. The hanger on them will hold the wire needed to attach them to the circle.

Fig. 3-1. Some ideas for brightening up your holidays.

On all pine cones, paint the inside edges with white paint about ½" down. When paint is dry, go over edges with glue and sprinkle with snowflake glitter.

To assemble, begin in the center of the circle. Wire the smaller pine cones, twisting the wire so that the pine cone will stand up straight.

Do the same with the other small cones, arranging them around the center as shown (Fig. 3-2). Attach the larger cones in the same manner, but between the others so that they reach to the outer rim of the circle.

At the end of every other small cone, wire a red ball. Between every other large pine cone, wire the green balls. The space left at the end of the red balls is where you will wire the holly and mistletoe to complete the decoration. A large red bow at the top will finish it off. Tie a red string to attach the decoration to the door.

ANGEL WALL DECORATION

Use felt or velour paper in turquoise about 18" × 12". Make a ½" hem at the bottom and top. Enlarge the pattern on brown wrapping paper. Make a tracing of the face, neck, hands and feet. Trace these onto pink felt. Trace the complete dress and wings on white felt. Trace hair on the yellow felt. Cut out and glue in place on velour paper. Stripes and scallops as well as some solid areas may be traced on any color you desire, and then glued in place over the gown. The largest circles may be cut from felt or maybe large beads or buttons that have been sewed on. The middle size circles are beads and the smallest represent sequins. The halo may be cut from gold lamé and glued on or made of solid gold beads.

Spray paint two ¼" × 10" dowel sticks gold. Insert in the hem at top and bottom. Tie the cord on the top dowel for hanging (Fig. 3-3).

BELL PULL FOR CHRISTMAS

Felt is a good material to use for this project as the sides do not have to be hemmed. A good size is 5" × 40". The top of the bell pull is usually hemmed to allow a ¼" dowel stick to be inserted to hang it. Dowel can be colored if you desire. A white or *ecru* color makes a good background color for most Christmas designs. Divide the

Fig. 3-2. Christmas wreath for the door.

Fig. 3-3. Pattern for the angel wall decoration.

40" into 10 areas which will be 4" each. The top block loses some of its size when you hem it. and the bottom is cut into a "V" shape about halfway up and slit into thin fringe-like strips.

Enlarge the patterns of both designs and letters. There are two ways to decorate your bell pull. You can cut the patterns from colored felt and, using a waterproof glue, glue them on, or you can use permanent marking pens or fabric paint to color them (Fig. 3-4).

Fig. 3-4. Bell pull for Christmas.

CHRISTMAS WINDOW DECORATION

Use the rims of two plastic lids—one the size of a whipped cream container and one about 4" in diameter. Cut strips of gold metallic paper and wrap both rings. Wrap diagonally for a smoother finish. Tie the two rings together at the top. Make a flower of red metallic paper—slitting in toward the center and scotch taping one petal a little over the other to give the flower shape.

Paste some glitter in the center. With thin floral wire, put a small silver ball through the center. Leave enough wire to go around a small branch of plastic holly, a spray of silver fringe and to tie to the top of the rings.

Make a small red ribbon bow. Attach a small dove to the top and tie around rings. Using the wire, attach the flower, holly and silver fringe around the bow and twist in back. Add a thin piece of ribbon to hang it (Fig. 3-5).

CANDLESTICK HOLDERS

Use three to four empty jars of varying sizes with lids on. Glue interesting arrangements on top of one another. Do not cap the top jar.

The top jar will hold your candle. A lid from a spray paint can works well.

Use felt cutouts or seals, paint, rickrack, or braid to decorate. Apply glue for fastening to jars (Figs. 3-6 and 3-7).

FOAM BALL CHRISTMAS DECORATION

Get friends to save for you small cream containers that are obtained in restaurants. You will need 50 of them.

Start with a 4" styrofoam ball. Glue a hanger into it so that it can be hung on a tree.

Put some glitter—red, green, blue or whatever color you wish to use—into a saucer. Put some white glue in another saucer. Dip each cup rim first into the glue and then into the glitter, rimming each cup with glitter.

When all cups have been glittered and are dry, insert a fairly long pin through a sequin of the same color as the glitter and into the center of the cup, pinning them to the ball.

Start at the top going around the holder. If you wish, you can put a cup at the top before you put the hanger in. It will take about five to go around the top. The next rows will go between each one in the row above and so forth until you reach the bottom where you will put one again (Fig. 3-8).

Fig. 3-5. The Christmas window decoration.

Fig. 3-6. A candlestick holder made with jars.

Fig. 3-7. Another attractive candlestick holder.

KISSING RING

Use two of the same size embroidery hoops and wrap with gold ribbon. Force one inside the other and tie in place. Put a gold bow at the top.

Use one smaller hoop to hang inside of the larger ones. Wrap this with gold ribbon and hang from the center of the larger one with a silver ball between them. String a silver ball from the bottom of that hoop. From the bottom of large hoops, hang a bow with three tiny silver balls and silver ribbon at different levels. Between the bow at the bottom and hoop, tie some mistletoe. Decorate the outside of hoops with beads and sequins or tiny bows (Fig. 3-9).

Fig. 3-8. Foam ball Christmas decoration.

MILKWEED POD ANGEL

Take a thin slab of wood from a 2" log. Glue a dried milkweed pod on its end to the slab. Carefully paint the inside of the milkweed pod with gold paint.

Glue a miniature angel in the inside of the pod where the pod is glued to the wood. Add small pieces of artificial greens by gluing them around the pod.

You can also take the milkweed pod and glue the angel inside to the base of the pod. Carefully stick a hole through the top of the pod and attach a lightweight cord. Hang as an ornament from the Christmas tree (Fig. 3-10).

GEM TREE

Choose a small artificial tree that you may have in your Christmas box, or use a branch from one of your trees or shrubs. Choose one that has a lot of twigs.

Cut strips from scraps of material or use old neckties cut in half. Wind them around each twig and the trunk. Be sure to remove lining before using ties.

Sink the covered branch into a 4" or 5" flower pot filled with earth. For a stronger base, you can use plaster of paris. Another good base is a brick with a hole drilled in the center. You can cover the branch with fabric if you wish.

Fig. 3-9. Kissing ring.

Fig. 3-10. Milkweed pod angel.

Find some old costume jewelry from garage sales, second-hand shops or from your family. Attach the gems to the branches of the tree. Gold safety pins can be used underneath the gems for fastening.

Many folks make the gem tree from their family gems. It makes for a meaningful conversation piece on the window sill or coffee table (Fig. 3-11).

DELLA ROBBIA WREATH

Use a wreath form or form one of privet hedge. Form a circle and fasten the ends with a piece of wire, using pliers to make it firm.

Cut bunches of boxwood or evergreen and tie onto the wreath base with green string. Keep the wreath full and balanced.

On top of the evergreen base, wire fresh kumquats, small love apples, and cranberries at intervals that you have shellacked and let dry. The Della Robbia wreath looks well hanging on the newel post and in the middle of the dining table with a candle in the center at holiday time (Fig. 3-12).

PINE CONE CHRISTMAS TREE

Take an 8" square piece of chicken wire. Mold it into the shape of an evergreen tree.

Mix up some plaster of paris and cover the wire. Let it harden. Put the tree on an old saucer and cover it with plaster of paris so it will have a sturdy base.

When completely dry, varnish the tree with dark stain. Let it dry.

Glue tiny pine cones as close together as possible all around the tree. Glue one on the top for the star. Arrange greens around the base as a centerpiece. These trees last a long time and are good for gift giving (Fig. 3-13).

SWEDISH KISSING BALL

Blow up an oval type ballon. Cut strips of paper 5" or 6" long, 1" wide. Soak them in flour paste (mix water with flour until you have a paste). Using your hands, cover a section of the balloon with paste and cover with strips of moistened paper strips as smoothly as possible. Cover the complete balloon. Let it dry thoroughly.

Fig. 3-11. Gem tree.

Fig. 3-12. Della Robbia wreath.

Then varnish the balloon with dark varnish. Let this dry well.

Glue with strong glue seed pods, cones, acorns, kernels of corn and anything interesting. You will have to do a section of the ball and allow it to dry every day until the ball is covered with decorations.

When dry, stick a piece of wire or paper clip with ends pulled out into the top of the ball so it holds *papier-maché*. Tie a red ribbon around a hook and hang it up in your window. This is really a holiday craft, but it is so attractive that folks hang it up all year round as a conversation piece (Fig. 3-14).

CHRISTMAS BELLS FROM PAPER CUPS

Paper cups from the five and ten store are fine for this project. Just do not pull out handles, if they have them. Spray paint the inside of the cup and the top rim with gold. Cover the outside of the cups with metallic paper, whatever color you wish. Make a pattern first by using typewriter paper to wrap around the cup. Add a strip of gold cord through the top of the cup with a small gold bell on the end. Tie three of these together with a red ribbon and bow. Hang them on your door (Fig. 3-15).

TRIPLE CANDLE HOLDER

Find a log in the woods about 8" long and 4" thick. Glue on the underside at either end a small piece of wood for balancing.

Glue three holes equidistant on the top of the log. Fill the holes with three red or green candles. These candle logs make nice centerpieces and window decorations (Fig. 3-16).

DOOR HANDLE COVER

Cut a 4 × 4 piece of red felt. Draw together with fine elastic so it will fit over the door handle and sew securely. Decorate with sequins and beads. Attach a red ribbon around the outside of the elastic and hang small brass bells into the ribbon (Fig. 3-17).

CHRISTMAS TREE ORNAMENT

Use a plastic lid at least 3" in diameter. Trace the design onto paper and color in the black areas. Trace onto a plastic lid using carbon paper.

Fig. 3-13. Pine cone Christmas tree.

Fig. 3-14. Swedish kissing ball.

Cut out the outline and all black areas. Spray one side with glue and sprinkle with silver or gold glitter. Allow to set for a few minutes and then shake off the excess. Turn to the other side and repeat. Put a hole for hanging in the top with a heated needle (Fig. 3-18).

HALLOWEEN MOBILE

You can trace these designs or enlarge them according to how big you wish your mobile to be. You will need to cut out the eye of the witch, the eyes, nose and mouth of the cat, and the little eyes and mouth of the bat.

In back of the witch's eye, paste the white of the eye and a green pupil. In the back of the cat, paste a yellow eye with a green pupil and a yellow nose and mouth. In back of the bat, one yellow piece will cover the eyes and mouth. In order for these not to show as the mobile turns, you will have to cover the other side the same as the front.

Fig. 3-15. Christmas bells made from paper bells.

With the skull, color the eyes and nose black. Outline the teeth and cheek line with black. Since the back of the skull will not show the eyes, nose and mouth, it does not have to be double.

Fig. 3-16. This holder can accommodate three candles.

Fig. 3-17. The door handle cover.

Fig. 3-18. Plastic snowflake for the Christmas tree.

Fig. 3-19. A ghost for the Halloween mobile.

Fig. 3-20. A witch for the Halloween mobile.

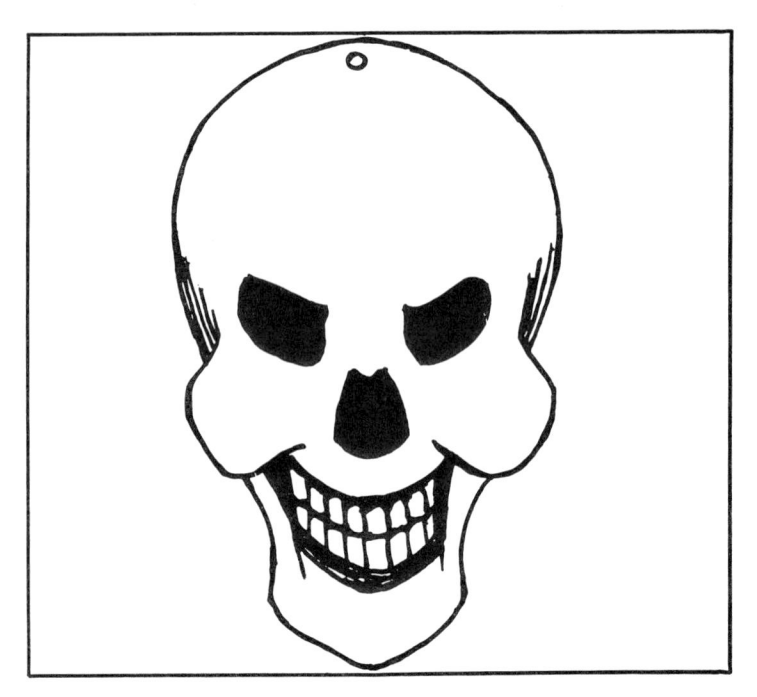

Fig. 3-21. A skull for the Halloween mobile.

Fig. 3-22. A cat for the Halloween mobile.

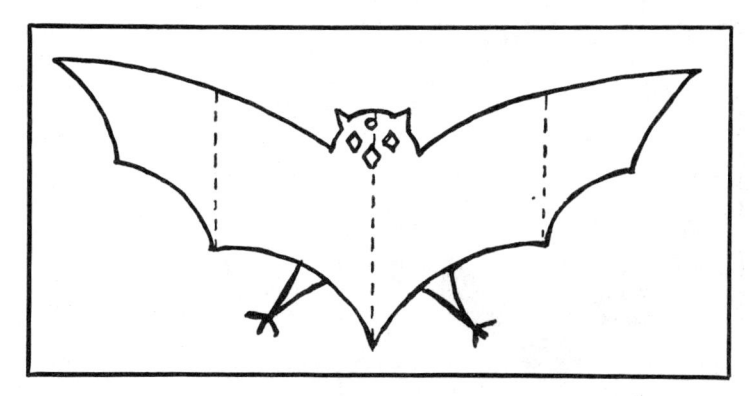

Fig. 3-23. A bat for the Halloween mobile.

Fig. 3-24. The finished Halloween skeleton.

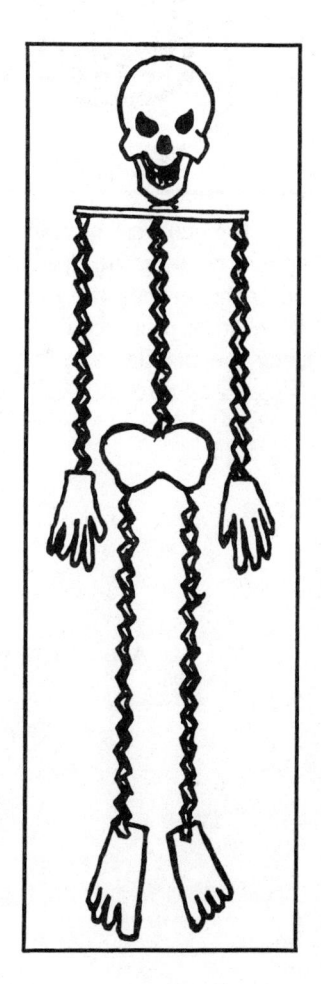

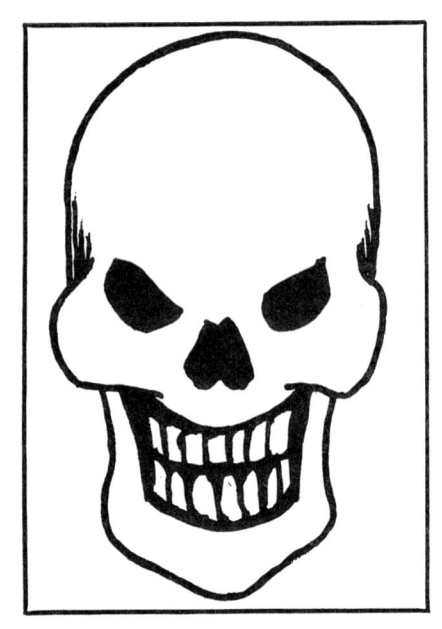

Fig. 3-25. The skull for the Halloween skeleton.

The ghost can be made in two ways. One way is like the skull, by just coloring the eye and mouth black but on both sides. The other way to make the ghost is to cover a small styrofoam ball with white crepe paper, color the mouth black and add movable eyes. To hang the mobile, see the illustrations for the butterfly mobile (Figs. 3-19 through 3-23).

Fig. 3-26. A hand for the Halloween skeleton.

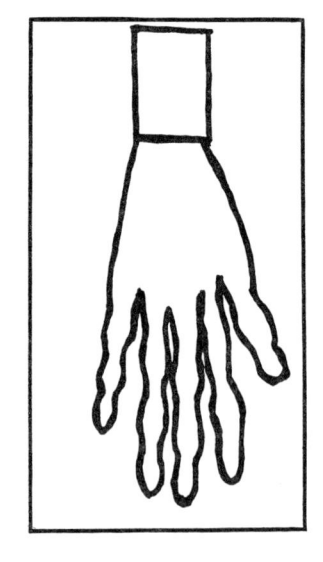

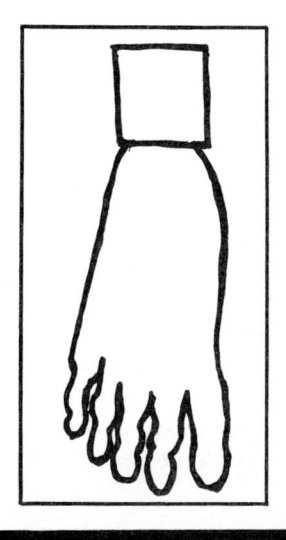

Fig. 3-27. A foot for the Halloween skeleton.

HALLOWEEN SKELETON

Trace the head, hands (one left and one right) and feet (one left and one right) on white paper and cut out (Figs. 3-24 through 3-28). Color in black areas on the head with black paint or crayon. Trace the pelvis on lightweight cardboard and the shoulder on heavy cardboard. Cut them out (Fig. 3-29). Cut two 4" × ½" strips of white paper for the neck. Cut two 8" × ½" strips for the torso and four 9" strips for the legs and arms.

Following Fig. 3-30A, paste one end of the neck strip over the other at the top. Figure 3-30B shows the right piece folded over the left. Figure 3-30C shows the bottom folded up. Figure 3-30D shows the top left folded over the right. Figure 3-30E shows the top pieces folded down. Continue in this manner until the neck piece is used up, pasting the last piece down. Fold the tab on the head under and on top of the neck. Paste the cardboard shoulder

Fig. 3-28. Hip for the Halloween skeleton.

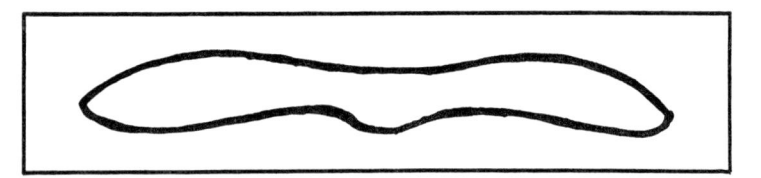

Fig. 3-29. Shoulder for the Halloween skeleton.

onto the bottom of the neck in the middle so it appears flat from top view.

Fold strips for the torso the same as the neck. Paste the top underneath the shoulder and the bottom to the tab on the hip in the middle.

Fold strips of arms and legs the same as the torso. Attach the arms to the shoulder and the legs to each side of the pelvis. Add hands and feet.

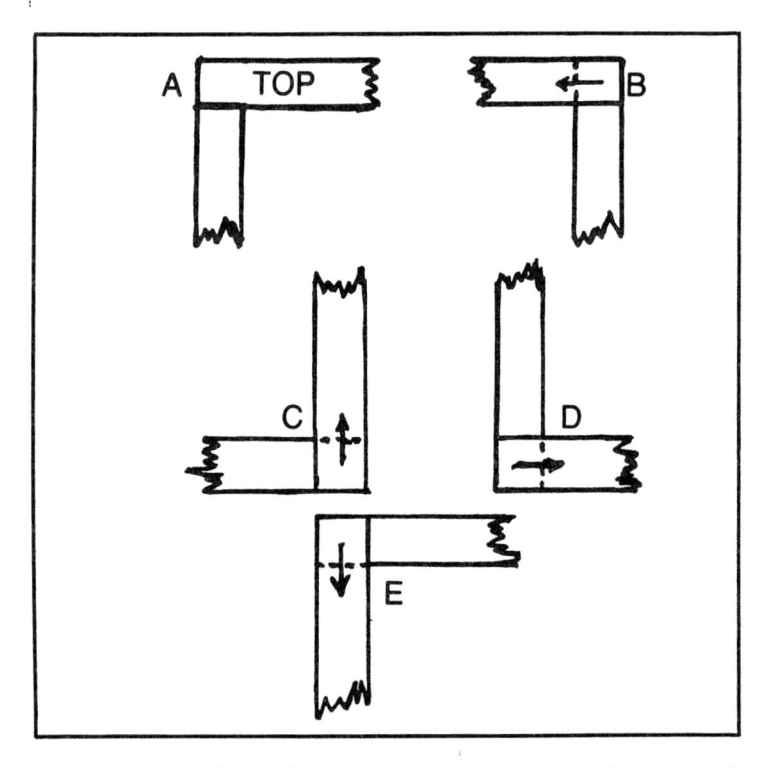

Fig. 3-30. Assembly for the skeleton's legs, arms and spine. (A) Paste one end of the neck strip over the other at the top. (B) The right piece is folded over the left. (C) The bottom is folded up. (D) The top left piece is folded over the right. (E) The top pieces folded down.

PUMPKIN FUN

Choose a round pumpkin. You can draw his face with a magic marker or carve his face with a paring knife. Be sure to cut off the top of the pumpkin, leaving the stem. Use as a lid. Dig out the insides of the pumpkin. Save the seeds, letting them dry on a tray. Use them for necklaces, seed pictures or roast them for eating. Place a candle in the body of the pumpkin and light it on Halloween night (Fig. 3-31).

EGG TREE

Choose about 10 raw eggs. Carefully take an ice pick and puncture a hole in either end of the raw egg. Blow out the contents into a saucer and use for cake making.

Decorate the egg shells with bits of rickrack, felt, feathers. tiny buttons, bits of lace and fur. If you wish, paint designs on the eggs and add faces, fancy hats and outfits.

Hang the eggs by a colored string or ribbon which is tied around a small twig inserted at the top of the egg onto a piece of driftwood. The driftwood is sunk in a pot of sand.

Every year you can bring out your egg tree at Easter time if you carefully wrap each egg in tissue paper and store in a box. Duck eggs and bantam eggs are unusual and fun to work with (Fig. 3-32).

EGG STAND

Take a small wooden ring and glue three big wooden beads on equal distance from each other. Let dry. Turn the ring around so it sits on the legs.

Fig. 3-31. This pumpkin will greet trick-or-treaters on Halloween night.

Fig. 3-32. Egg tree.

Fit the decorated egg into the center hold of the ring. Tinkertoy beads left over from baby toys work well. So do wooden rings from curtains and drapes (Fig. 3-33).

KITCHEN WITCH

Take an old silk stocking. Fill it with soft cotton, starting with the head. Take tucks in the face to make the head look like a witch. Form a long nose. Take a tuck, sink two holes above the nose for the eyes. Pull down and sew a tuck for the mouth. Add movable eyes or two black buttons for eyes and glue red felt for a mouth. Gather a tuck on either side of the mouth and form a chin underneath the mouth by moving around the cotton batting.

Fig. 3-33. Egg stand.

Fig. 3-34. Kitchen witch.

Fig. 3-35. Plastic tomato basket decoration.

Tie a tight cord around the neck and start forming the body. At the bottom of the body, divide the hose and stuff two legs. The witch can be 8" to 12" long. Make flesh colored fabric feet, sewing indentations for five toes. Pad and sew to the legs.

Cut two strips of hose 4" long. Sew, stuff and attach to the upper part of the body for arms.

Take some fabric and drape around the body for a dress held at the middle with a sash. Make a triangular scarf for the head and tie around the head for a covering.

Fig. 3-36. Christmas centerpiece.

Fig. 3-37. Winter centerpiece.

Find a stick 12" long and on one end tie bits of a broom tightly. Place the stick between the witch's legs. Hang her up in the kitchen (Fig. 3-34).

PLASTIC TOMATO BASKET DECORATION FOR A DOOR

The long thin plastic baskets that tomatoes come in are good for this craft. Starting at the short end with red ribbon that is as wide as the small openings in the side of the basket, lace the ribbon under the middle plastic upright over the corner and into the first opening in the side. Continue around the basket by going in and out until you reach the beginning. Scotch tape the end to the beginning.

Fig. 3-38. An attractive styrofoam egg decoration for Easter.

Scotch tape two strips of red ribbon the same width over the end pieces. Bring the two strips from each side together at the top with a bow. Make it long enough to hang.

Fill the basket with artificial fruits and nuts, adding a few pieces of holly or long needled pine. If you do not like the color of the basket, spray paint first, or use permanent marking pens or nail polish (Fig. 3-35).

CHRISTMAS CENTERPIECE

Cover a box with brick type paper. Use a Santa Claus made of *chenile* that you find in a quarter dollar store. You can also use one cut from a magazine or make one using cardboard. Perch the Santa Claus on the edge of the chimney. Then fill the box with small presents or Christmas candy (Fig. 3-36).

WINTER TIME CENTERPIECE

Sort all the seashells you have collected at the seashore. Arrange them in a pretty container and stick straw flowers in between the shells. The flowers will bring out the colors of the shells (Fig. 3-37).

FANCY EASTER EGGS

Buy egg-shaped styrofoam eggs (large ones). Decorate them with sequins or beads. Glue rickrack around the four sides of the

Fig. 3-39. Hang the decoration up with a ribbon.

Fig. 3-40. Broom corn swag.

eggs using proper glue. Hang the decoration up by a pretty ribbon in your window for Easter (Figs. 3-38 and 3-39).

BROOM CORN SWAG

Gather a bunch of broom corn together and tie tightly around an old broomstick measuring 1½ feet long. Trim off bristles. At the top of the stick, arrange some artificial flowers and tie with a gay colored ribbon. Hang on a cup hook on your front door with the broom head facing down (Fig. 3-40).

Chapter 4
Party Projects

We all enjoy parties, but sometimes they can turn out to be a little dull. Make sure yours are always sparkling affairs and happy events.

Add some centerpieces, decorations and favors. Youngsters especially enjoy something they can take home with them as a momento (Fig. 4-1).

CHRISTMAS SLEIGH

The size of the sleigh depends on how big a box you use to work over. Draw a red *bristol board* the two sides of the sleigh as shown (Fig.4-2). Paste to the sides of the box (Fig. 4-3).

The back and front are also red bristol board, but of a thinner quality. They are the width of the box, with tabs added where indicated in Fig. 4-2 and curled around. The curl at the back is pasted to the middle of the back of the sleigh.

The coils and runners can be made from heavy cardboard or reed and spray painted silver. Glue to the bottom of the box. Place small gifts in the sleigh, wrapped and tied with a ribbon reaching out across the table to each guest.

CHOIRBOYS FOR CHRISTMAS

Choirboys' bodies are made the same as the angel, but instead of a 6" radius for the gown make it 4". Cut a piece of lace paper doily about 2" wide for the collar, and paste it around the neck so that it sticks out a little. The gown should be black. Cut arms about 2" long. Add hands, but paste each end to a small piece of white folded

Fig. 4-1. Here are some items which will lead to successful parties.

paper for music. Use a smaller foam ball for the head and black strips for hair (Fig. 4-4).

STANDING ANGEL

Cut from white paper a half circle 9″ in diameter. Make a small half circle in the middle of the flat side about 1″ in diameter.

Fig. 4-2. View of the sleigh.

161

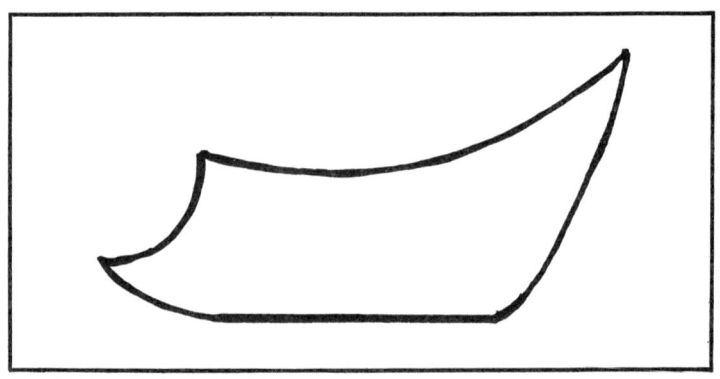

Fig. 4-3. Inner box for the sleigh.

Cut arms and wings according to the pattern shown from white paper. Cut two hands from pink paper.

Fold a large half circle to form a cone which is the angel's gown. Make sure the wings are cut so they will be opposites. Paste the tab to the robe in back.

Paste arms slightly to the back and almost touching in front. Paste hands inside arms at the bottom in an attitude of prayer, and then paste together.

Halo is made of thin floral wire, the circle part covered by wrapping it with yellow swiss straw. When the angel is assembled,

Fig. 4-4. Choirboy favor.

Fig. 4-5. Standing angel favor.

place a foam ball on top for the head. Paint it pink or cover with pink crepe paper.

Cut several strips of yellow paper for hair about 4" long and some about 1". Curl one end tightly with scissors. Curl the other end slightly to go over the top of the head. Short pieces are for bangs in front. Glue wire that is not covered with swiss straw into the back of head, and glue the head to the top of the robe (Fig. 4-5).

SUGAR PLUM TREE

Cut a branch from an evergreen tree or just a plain branch. Sink it into a bucket of earth. Cover the bucket with red paper to make it attractive.

Tie sweet treats like ribbon candy, Christmas candy, cutout cookies, strings of popcorn, lollipops, big foiled hershey buds and chocolate foil Santa Clauses on the branches with red ribbon.

At the bottom of the tree, tie a small scissor with a red ribbon. Every child that leaves the house at holiday time may cut his sweet treat from the tree (Fig. 4-6).

PLASTIC SNOWMAN

Find an empty bleach bottle with no handle. Fill it half full of sand. Spread glue over the plastic bottle and cover with cotton batting. As you wind the batting around the bottle, stitch neatly where the cotton joins.

At the neck of the bottle, stick a large styrofoam ball onto the neck. Glue black buttons on the face for eyes and nose. Use a piece of red felt for the mouth.

Take 4″ of batting and roll them in a cylinder shape. Sew them to the chest of the snowman for arms.

At the quarter dollar store find a small plastic red hat. Stick a feather in it and put it on the snowman's head. Tie a small scarf around the neck (Fig. 4-7).

CHRISTMAS NUT CUP

Cover a small cupcake paper cup with pink paper. On one side paste a small red circle for a nose in the middle. Paste two movable

Fig. 4-6. Sugar plum tree.

Fig. 4-7. The snowman can be used as a doorstop.

eyes above as shown in Fig. 4-8. Cut a mustache from white paper and paste under the nose. Beneath that put a small round or oval red mouth. Cut strips of white paper about ¼" wide and 1" long for a

Fig. 4-8. Christmas nut or candy cup.

Fig. 4-9. Christmas place card.

beard below the mouth. Curl and paste on. Allow the strips to get longer as you proceed to go around the entire cup for the hair. Make a red paper cone to cover the top of the cup for the hat. Add a small

Fig. 4-10. The pinata is a popular party item.

Fig. 4-11. The pink swan is needed for the valentine centerpiece.

cotton ball on top. Add little circles of white paper all around the edge of the hat so you can take it off.

Fig. 4-12. The pine cone turkey.

167

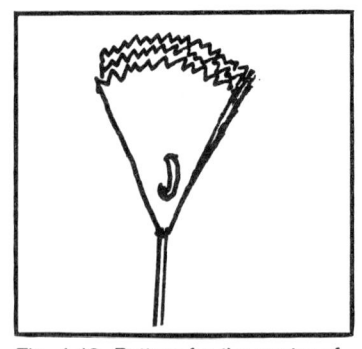

Fig. 4-13. Pattern for the center of the paper posy.

Fig. 4-14. Pattern for the first layer of petals.

PLACE CARDS

Fold a piece of colored construction paper measuring about 4" to 5" in two. On the top side draw a winter scene. Then paint with your brush or magic markers.

For a main point of interest, take some cotton balls or make small balls of cotton. Use two for a snowman's body and one for his head.

Make him a black paper hat and glue it to the top of his head. Take a bit of red ribbon and wrap it around his neck for the scarf. Put some dots of Elmer's glue and sprinkle glitter on them. This makes it look like snow. Add the names of the guests at your dining table (Fig. 4-9).

PINATA

Buy a very large heavy weight balloon. Tie tightly when it is as large as you can blow it up. Use 3" wide crepe paper of any color for the first three coats. Cut each piece about 6" or 8" long and

Fig. 4-15. Pattern for the second layer of petals.

Fig. 4-16. The flower has been put together.

paste all over the balloon. If you paste in a criss-cross manner, it will be smoother. Cover the balloon with at least three coats.

Now using whatever color you want the boy's suit to be, start at the top and go around, making a circle. Fluff the edges by spreading. Keep on covering the base with circles, each a little bigger than the other and pasted under the last one. Do this until the entire balloon is covered with fluffy crepe paper.

Cut out a circle from the bottom large enough to place small gifts in. Never mind that it spoils your crepe paper. After you have placed enough gifts in for every child who will participate in opening the pinata, you will replace the piece you cut out, adding more crepe paper to cover where it was cut.

To make this a little simpler, the arms and legs are single pieces of paper pasted under the frills. The head can be a small balloon merely colored with permanent marking pens and tied to

Fig. 4-17. Valentine candy cut.

Fig. 4-18. The clown egg head.    Fig. 4-19. The princess egg head.

the top of the body or glued. You can add a paper cone for a hat, yarn for hair and paper ears if you wish. Hang the pinata in the middle of the room (Fig. 4-10).

VALENTINE CENTERPIECE

You will need a box about 10" × 7" as the base for the pink swan. Paint the box pink on the outside.

Draw two sides of the swan as shown in Fig. 4-11, but make the rear and front a little longer than they would naturally be. This extra length will appear shorter, because you are going to paste them together at the front and rear. Paste over the box, bringing

Fig. 4-20. The Chinaman egg head.    Fig. 4-21. The lion egg head.

170

Fig. 4-22. The chicken is used for the Easter centerpiece.

them together at the head and tail. Paint pink, with a black eye and yellow beak.

The open area in the front and back of the swan can be filled in with crumpled newspaper. When filled out, cover with pink crepe paper. Cut large feathers of pink crepe paper and paste on top of the sides, allowing an occasional end to stick out like a real feather.

If possible, when completed place it on a mirror to simulate water or colored paper. Place valentine cards in the box with strings attached for each guest.

PINE CONE TURKEY

Select one large pine cone for the body and one small one for the turkey's head. Attach them together with a brown pipe cleaner. Dip the pipe cleaner in coffee to color it brown.

Make small legs by cutting the pipe cleaner about 1" long. Glue them to the bottom of the body.

Use red construction paper and make a fan-like tail, gluing it to the back of the body cone. Glue pine cone petals over the tail. Also cut two pieces of small red paper on the side of the pine cone head. These turkeys make nice Thanksgiving favors and centerpieces (Fig. 4-12).

PAPER POSY

Take a facial tissue, open it, and refold it lengthwise. Cut the folded edge off neatly. Fold the strip as if you were making a fan. Be sure to make each fold ¾" wide.

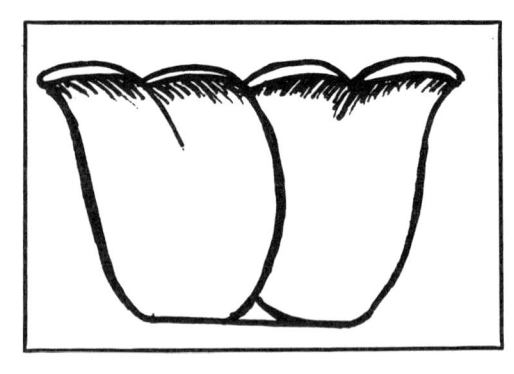

Fig. 4-23. Easter candy cup.

When you have them all folded, use a staple in the center and then begin to separate the layers of tissues until they look like a flower. These paper flowers can decorate for weddings, Mother's Day and arrangements (Figs. 4-13 through 4-16).

VALENTINE CANDY CUP

Enlarge the pattern and trace onto red construction paper. Cut out. Do not cut where hearts are attached at the sides or you will cut all four hearts apart. Fold where they are attached together, folding the tab under the last heart. Trace four smaller hearts on pink paper and paste in the middle of the red heart. Ruffle a narrow strip of white crepe paper or use the outside of a lace doily to put an edge on the large hearts. Place hearts around a paper cup. Cut a small piece of dental stick long enough to reach to the bottom of the heart on one side and to stick out the top on the other side. Trace a

Fig. 4-24. Halloween witch favor.

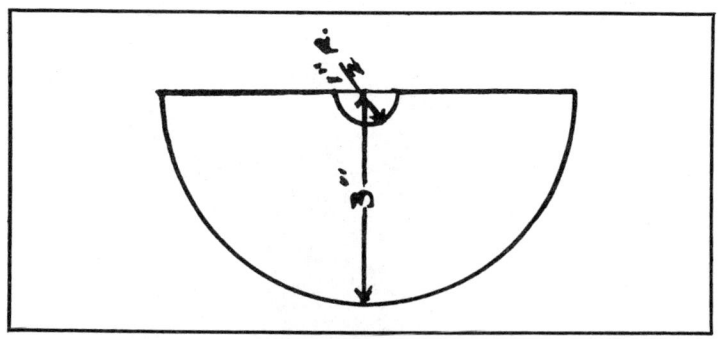

Fig. 4-25. Pattern for the witch's cape.

pattern of arrow head and feather end of white paper and paste on, or if you like you can use a real feather. Insert the heart as shown (Fig. 4-17). Write the names of guests on the pink heart.

EGG HEADS

Boil eggs until you are sure they are hard-boiled. You can decorate them with paint or colored paper. For the clown, leave the egg white. Give him a wide red mouth and two blue diamond shapes for eyes with a black dot in the center. The nose can be a round red ball. Make ears from white paper and paste on. Use bright orange pieces of yarn, gluing from the center out (Fig. 4-18).

For the princess the face may be dyed pink if you like. Paint eyes white with blue pupils. Use a marking pen to make the mouth and line for the nose. Cut ¼" strips of yellow construction paper for hair about 3" long. Curl the bottom end up and make a slight curl the opposite way to fit the top of the head. Start at the sides and glue from the top of the head. Cut smaller pieces for bangs. You can

Fig. 4-26. Halloween nut cup.

Fig. 4-27. Prune and marshmallow favor.

make a hat for her with a feather in it or a crown from gold paper for a queen (Fig. 4-19).

For the Chinaman, you can use a brown egg. Use marking pens for his features. Use the same color of paper for ears and cut a long black mustache. Make a *coolie hat* of brown paper. Cut a circle

Fig. 4-28. Walnut shell bouquet favor.

Fig. 4-29. Corsage favor.

about 3" in diameter and make a slit as shown to center. Overlap and glue. His hair will not show in front, but in back you can use a few thin strips of black paper, pasted close to his head and to a point in back at the bottom. There you can add a thin strip for a pigtail (Fig. 4-20).

To make the lion, use a black marking pen for around the eyes and mouth, but use pink for the nose. Cut large ears from white paper, coloring the inner part pink. You can add whiskers by using thin strips of white paper or making pin holes and inserting plastic bristles from a brush (Fig. 4-21).

To make the stands for your egg heads, make a circle of stiff paper 4" in diameter with an inner circle of 1½" in diameter. Slash

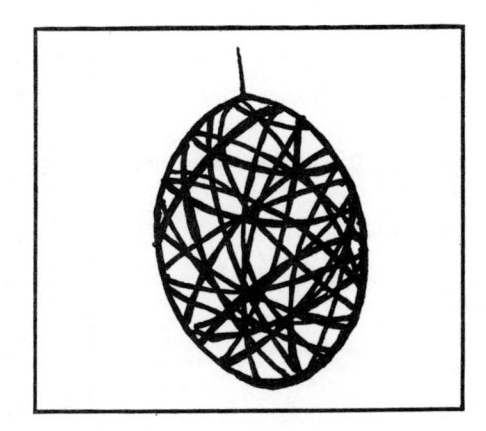

Fig. 4-30. Fancy balloon.

Fig. 4-31. Thanksgiving centerpiece.

on the dotted line. Glue one end of the circle under the other to form a collar shape. The egg will sit on this.

EASTER CENTERPIECE

The Easter centerpiece is made exactly the same as the valentine centerpiece, with the exception of the color and feathers.

Fig. 4-32. Construction of the man's shoulder.

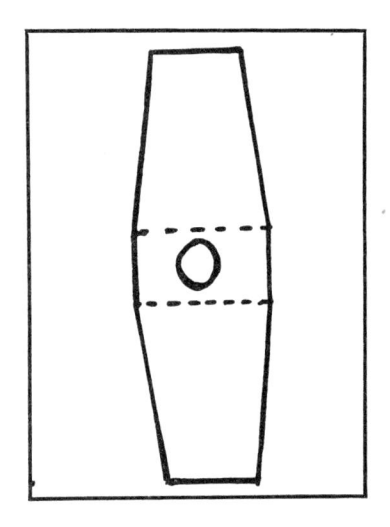

Fig. 4-33. The completed scarecrow.

The two sides of the chicken are pasted to the sides of the box, brought together in the front and back, but use white paper. When adding the white crepe paper feathers, make them smaller than you did with the swan. Paste them so that they stick out a little more, making the chicken look a little ruffled. Add red comb, wattles and black eyes.

Place this centerpiece on the green cellophane fluff that is used inside Easter baskets. Fill the box with colored and decorated Easter eggs (Fig. 4-22).

EASTER CANDY CUP

Use colored crepe paper, the color of the tulip. Cut six petals the size and shape of Fig. 4-23. Spread crepe paper at the bottom and make the base of the petal look bulbous. Curl the top of the petals over by rolling over a pencil.

177

Fig. 4-34. The umbrella for the bridal shower centerpiece.

Paste petals overlapping each other and to the bottom of the candy cup. You may need to paste petals together a little where they overlap.

HALLOWEEN FAVOR

The standing witch favor is made of black construction paper (Fig. 4-24). On a sheet that is 9" × 12", draw a half circle as indicated in Fig. 4-25. A 3" half circle and a 1¼" quarter circle will be her dress, cape and part of her hat.

Cut all three out, and on the two half circles cut a half circle in the middle of the top to go around her neck. Paste the large circle together to form her dress. On the 3" circle, punch two holes where indicated to tie the cape around her neck.

Fig. 4-35. Bridal shower place mats.

178

Fig. 4-36. The stork for the baby shower centerpiece.

On another piece of black paper, cut a 2″ circle with a ¾″ circle inside it. Slash the inner circle. Do not cut out. Curl both ends of the quarter circle to aid in pasting it together to form a cone for the top of her hat. Do not overlap edges any more than you have to in order to paste. Place this on top of the brim, folding the slashed edges up inside, and paste.

Use a small styrofoam ball for the head and almost completely cover with cotton for hair. Glue this to the top of the dress. Tie the cape around so that it stands out. Finish by gluing the hat on the head.

HALLOWEEN NUT CUP

Cut four pumpkins similar to Fig. 4-26. Cut out eyes, nose and mouth. Paste yellow paper behind the orange pumpkin and the green stem at the top. Paste each to the side of a small paper cup in the middle. Paste the edges of the pumpkins together around the cup.

Fig. 4-37. Gift holder-cradle for the baby shower centerpiece.

PRUNE AND MARSHMALLOW FAVOR

Take a marshmallow and stick a toothpick in the middle. On the toothpick place a prune.

Take a tiny bit of white frosting. With another toothpick, paint a face on the prune.

Use a bit of construction paper and make a tiny hat for the prune head. This is a cute favor (Fig. 4-27).

WALNUT SHELL BOUQUET

Clean out a walnut shell and use one half. Paint the inside with a colored enamel paint or gild it. Brush on some glue and sprinkle glitter.

Place some modeling clay in the center with your finger. You can use a drop of glue if you want to hold the clay to the shell.

Fig. 4-38. Baby shower crib favor.

Fig. 4-39. Circus tent for the youngsters' birthday party centerpiece.

Place in the clay a birthday candle, any small ceramic figure, an artificial flower, a tiny doll, a sparkling earring, shiny beads and a forest scene using weeds from the roadside. Attach on either side of the top of the walnut shell a ribbon or yarn handle with glue. These make cute favors for parties (Fig. 4-28).

CORSAGE FAVORS

Buy some artificial cloth leaves in a hobby or floral supply store. The leaves that are three on a branch are handy for corsage work.

Lay the leaves on the table and attach small artificial flowers or seed pods to the base of leaves with a thin piece of wire. After the corsage is as full as you wish, tie a ribbon of contrasting color in the center.

Trim off wires and cover with floristic tape. Stick a floristic pin into each stem of the corsage. These items make cute Christmas favors or gifts and package ornaments, using the material of the season (Fig. 4-29).

FANCY BALLOON

Blow up a balloon and tie the end tightly. Wind cord string around the balloon, criss-crossing until the whole balloon is covered. Leave the ends 6" long.

Pour liquid starch into a bowl. Set your balloon in the bowl and with a spoon pour starch over the string. Make sure all the string is well soaked.

Hang the balloon up to dry in a safe place. After the string is thoroughly dry, prick the balloon with a pin, carefully removing all pieces of broken balloon. Hang it up for a special party or for an ornament for your Christmas tree. You can also use it as a centerpiece for your table (Fig. 4-30).

THANKSGIVING CENTERPIECE

Use a tray for the middle of the table. Collect colored leaves and lay them on the bottom of the tray.

Construct a small cabin of popsicle sticks or cardboard. Paint it brown.

Create pilgrims out of construction paper and place them outside of the cabin. You can add animals, a garden and trees using small pieces of green sponge or construction paper.

You can place on the tray assorted pieces of fruit, oranges, a pineapple, grapefruit, nuts and bananas with a bunch of grapes on top. Do not forget the nutcracker.

The dolls for the centerpiece are made from black, brown and white construction paper (Fig. 4-31).

Fig. 4-40. This clown favor is made of stones.

Fig. 4-41. Make heavy cardboard numbers for the age of the birthday person.

The girl pilgrim is made from a cone of brown paper about 9" tall. Cut the top of the cone off so a small styrofoam ball can be glued to it. Her cape is also a cone shape about 4" long, with two holes at the top to tie around her neck. The collar is part of a white circle with the center cut out and pasted around the cape. The arms of both dolls are merely strips of paper pasted beneath the cape. Paste pink hands to the underside and paste together with a small strip of brown paper between, like a book.

The male pilgrim's shoulders are cut like Fig. 4-32, the wide part being the shoulders, with a hole cut for the head. His tunic is a cone shape with the top cut off to accommodate his waist, the front of which is pasted to the front of the tunic and the back to the back, with a black paper belt around the waist. His legs are two coils of the brown paper with tabs attached to paste under the tunic. His hat is brown and made like the witch's hat, but it doesn't come to a point. Add a white collar, arms, hands and a gun.

Arrange the figures in the center of long needle pine cones and holly. The faces of both dolls can be colored with styrofoam paint and permanent marking pens.

SCARECROW

Find an old pair of jeans, shirt and a hat. Stuff the shirt and pants with straw or old rags from the rag bag. Be sure to tie the pants with straw or old rags. Tie the wrists and the bottom of the jeans tightly with strong cord to hold stuffing.

Fasten jeans to the shirt, placing the scarecrow in a sitting position on a bench. Attach shoes for feet. Place stuffed gloves at the wrists for hands, using a strong cord.

Place a pumpkin head on the scarecrow's body. You may use a lady's stocking stuffed with stuffing. Tie it shut at the bottom for the head. Draw a face on the pumpkin or stocking.

Add a hat to finish the scarecrow. He is great as a Halloween greeter at your party (Fig. 4-33).

BRIDAL SHOWER CENTERPIECE AND PLACE MATS

For a centerpiece, you can use an umbrella upturned in the center of the table. It can be balanced by being surrounded with cotton batting covered with confetti.

On each rib place an artificial carnation, and from the handle hang "something new, something old or something blue." Gifts can be placed in the umbrella and around it if necessary (Fig. 4-34).

Make place mats of red construction paper. They are two hearts connected (Fig. 4-35).

For favors, you can buy inexpensive plastic champagne glasses. Tie a ribbon around the stem, with a magic marker put on the date of the shower. Hang fancy balloons that are made with all-white string or yarn around the home.

BABY SHOWER CENTERPIECE AND FAVORS

Make a centerpiece of a stork carrying a baby from heavy cardboard (Fig. 4-36). Use a lightweight doll for the baby and a piece of plain white material for the blanket. Make a hole in the beak of the stork to hold the blanket and baby. Tape on the other side. Insert the base of the stork into a slot that you have cut in a board. Cover the base with crepe paper or cotton.

Fig. 4-42. This pencil makes a neat party favor when it is decorated.

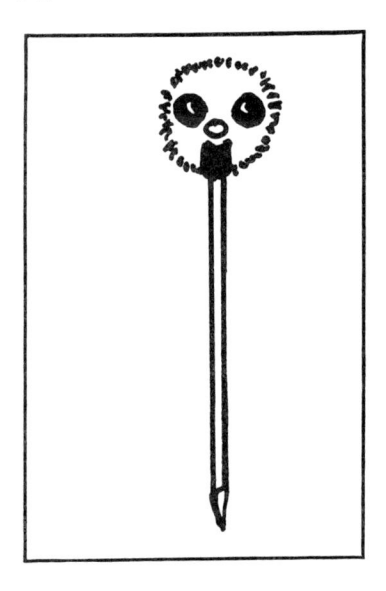

For place mats, cut a square of white paper to resemble a diaper. Pin a gold safety pin in one corner.

Favors can be cribs made of cardboard and toothpicks (Figs. 4-37 and 4-38). Cover some cotton batting with pink and blue crepe paper for a blanket. Fill with candy. Hang balloons around with names on them for the baby.

YOUNGSTERS'S BIRTHDAY PARTY CENTERPIECE AND FAVORS

Make a large circus tent from brown wrapping paper for a centerpiece. Put small flags on top of the toothpicks and paper. Fold back the front flaps for an opening to the tent. Place a sign above calling the circus by the name of whomever the party is for (Fig. 4-39). Place the tent on green paper for grass. Gifts may go inside and around it.

For place mats, use plain white construction paper. Find pictures in magazines of elephants, tigers, lions and horses. Paste them in the center.

Hang balloons on which you have pasted children's favorite cartoon characters or Walt Disney characters. If the children are a little older, you might paste teeneyboppers' favorite stars.

Favors can be clowns made of rocks (Fig. 4-40). Find a fairly large one for the head. Paint it white. Add movable eyes, a small red stone for the nose and paint the mouth on. You can add a fringe of artificial fur around the head for hair. Make a cone hat. Paint dots on it and get a very small pom-pom for the top. Give the clown two smaller stone feet glued to the bottom of his head. If you wish, you can use more stones and make a whole body, with pipe cleaner arms.

TEENAGERS' BIRTHDAY PARTY CENTERPIECE AND FAVORS

Rent a revolving light and place it above a table to give the appearance of a disco. For a centerpiece, make heavy cardboard numbers for the age of whomever the party is being given for (Fig. 4-41). Make a slit in a board wide enough to insert the cardboard so it will stand up. Paint the numbers in bright fluorescent colors in a wild design. The base can be covered with crepe paper and confetti, and the gifts placed around it.

Make place mats in the form of large records. Paint the center circle red and the outer one black. Print on a small piece of paper the names of each guest, and paste in the center of the record.

Hang fancy balloons that have been made with bright colored string or yarn around the room. Before hanging, insert in each one of them a prediction for each guest as to what he may become—president, rock star, professional athlete, movie star, banker, etc. Guests must pick a balloon and retrieve the prediction without wrecking the balloon.

For favors, glue a small pom-pom on the eraser end of a pencil. Glue two very small movable eyes on a smaller pom-pom for a nose. Give each guest two pencils—one in the form of a female, which can be distinguished from the male by a small lacy paper collar around the neck, and the other a male with a bow tie. Add a tiny red felt tongue which sticks out (Fig. 4-42).

Chapter 5
Crafts For Personal Enjoyment

So much satisfaction is derived from creating easy crafts for your own enjoyment. Working with one's hands is good therapy for the hustle and bustle of this busy old world. And the finished product may be used in your home or given as a gift with the knowledge that you had the pleasure in making the craft (Fig. 5-1).

BRICK DOORSTOP

Use a brick that you may have around the property, or buy one in a lumber mill. Lay the brick on a piece of scrap material that has bright colors and a tight weave. Measure the fabric larger than the brick.

Use a piece of chalk for marking. Then take scissors and cut the material.

Stitch three sides on the wrong side of material on the sewing machine, or use an embroidery needle and, with a button thread, overcast the sides. Turn the brick cover inside out so that the stitches are hidden on the inside.

Slip the brick into the cover. With small stitches, neatly close up the third side.

BELT HOLDER

Take a piece of scrap lumber about 6" to 8" long. Measure and draw pencil lines for sawing. Saw it 2½" to 3" wide, using wood ½" to ¾" thick.

Paint the lumber and decorate as you wish. You might use your name. When the paint is dry, screw cup hooks into the top of the board over the name.

Fig. 5-1. The making of these crafts will give you much personal satisfaction.

On either side of the top corner of the board, attach two more cup hooks. Tie a heavy cord to each hook for hanging on the closet door (Fig. 5-2).

PEACH STONE DUCKS

During the summer, save peach pits. Wash and dry thoroughly.

In a novelty store purchase small duck heads. Glue each duck head on the end of a peach stone. They make nice favors and can be used for knickknack shelves (Fig. 5-3).

OLD FASHIONED OIL LAMP

Find two oleo tubs of the pound size that do not have fancy curves in them and are the same size and shape. Glue one on top of the other, with the widest parts together.

Fig. 5-2. Belt holder.

Fig. 5-3. The peach stone duck.

Glue a small can, like a tuna fish can, to the bottom and one to the top. Inside the top can glue the lid of a spray paint can to hold the candle. A handle can be made by cutting a piece of tin or plastic, forming it into a ring and gluing to the upper portion of the lamp.

When everything is assembled, spray paint the entire lamp base with a flat black paint. Place a glass oil lamp globe on top and a candle in the lid of the spray can on top. This can be made colorful if you wish by adding a red ribbon and some artificial holly to the side (Fig. 5-4).

Fig. 5-4. The old fashioned oil lamp.

189

Fig. 5-5. The walnut shell sailboat.

WALNUT SHELL SAILBOAT

Clean half a walnut shell and smooth inside. Use two pieces of Q-tips. Take off the cotton ends. Cut one 3" long and one 1-¾" long. Drill two holes where indicated by dotted line in the bottom of the shell large enough to glue the Q-tips into. Cut sails according to pattern and glue at the top and bottom (Fig 5-5).

BURR PORCUPINE

Find a long seed pod like a burr. Attach four small shields from a pine cone and glue for legs to the underside of the burr. Glue two on the top of the head for ears.

For the face, glue on part of a dried weed, and on either side of the face glue movable eyes. For the tail, glue a small stick on the back of the body. These little porcupines make cute favors, Christmas tree ornaments or package ties (Fig. 5-6).

Fig. 5-6. The burr porcupine makes a neat ornament.

Fig. 5-7. Potato prints.

POTATO PRINTS

Place a white piece of paper on the table. Draw a simple design in outline on the paper, such as a leaf or flower.

Cut a potato in half and sketch on it the design you drew from the paper. Cut out around the design so it stands out. Press the potato onto a colored stamp pad. Then press the potato onto the paper and you will have your design. Potato printing makes nice notepaper and wrapping paper, using your monograms and special designs (Fig. 5-7).

MISTER POTATO HEAD

Bake a small potato in a slow oven at 200 degrees F. for about two hours. This will remove all the moisture.

Let the potato cool. Then stick a green garden stake or thin stick into one end of the potato just partway through.

Place sequins with pins or thumbtacks into the head for eyes. Take a knife and cut a nose and slit for the mouth. Break up a dry noodle and put it in place in the mouth for teeth. Glue some bits of wool on the head for hair.

Fig. 5-8. The potato head will last a long time.

Let the potato head dry near the heat. It will become hard as a rock and will last a long time (Fig. 5-8).

LAMBKIN

Buy a medium sized styrofoam ball, a small styrofoam egg, some white felt and some white rug yarn. Cover a small peanut can or small round cardboard box with white felt, gluing it onto the can or box.

Fig. 5-9. A cute little lamb.

Fig. 5-10. Treasure box.

Use one-half of a styrofoam egg-shaped ball. Cover with more white felt, leaving the end of the egg for the nose. Glue four pieces of styrofoam for legs about 3" long.

Glue two small black buttons for eyes on the face, and glue white felt ears on the side of the ball. Make small curls of white rug yarn by twisting in coils, cutting off extra yarn, and gluing them to the can or box until the body is completely covered. Do the same to the legs.

Allow a ½" piece of white yarn to dangle for the lamb's tail at the end of the box or can. Glue well (Fig. 5-9).

Fig. 5-11. Ice candle.

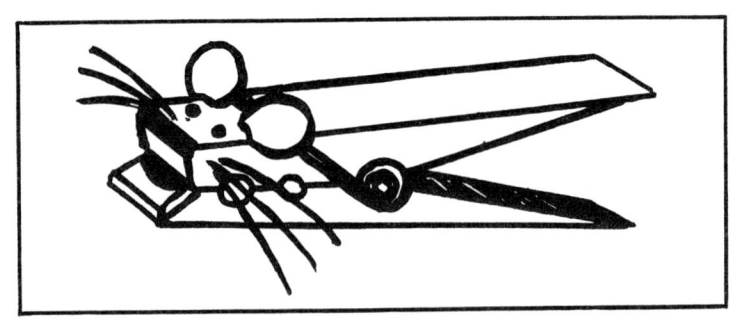

Fig. 5-12. A unique clothespin clip.

TREASURE BOX

Use an old tackle or small toolbox that you may find in the cellar. Be sure to scrub it well both inside and out. Let it dry well.

Sand off all rough spots. Paint with a bright colored enamel, inside and outside.

Decorate the box with pictures from seed catalogs, or draw your own designs. Glue them to the box and let things dry thoroughly.

Cover the box with clear varnish inside and outside. Spar varnish is good for preservaiton.

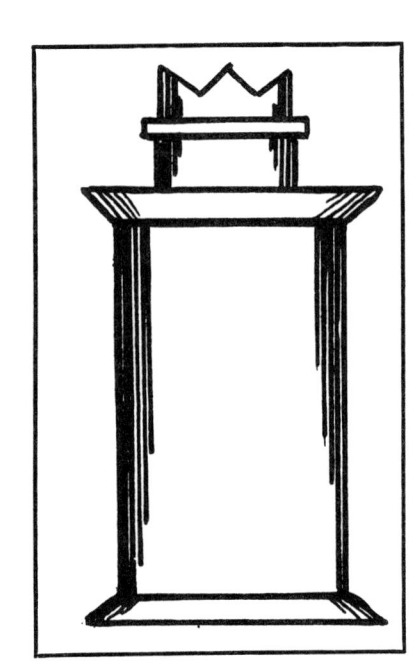

Fig. 5-13. The king chess piece.

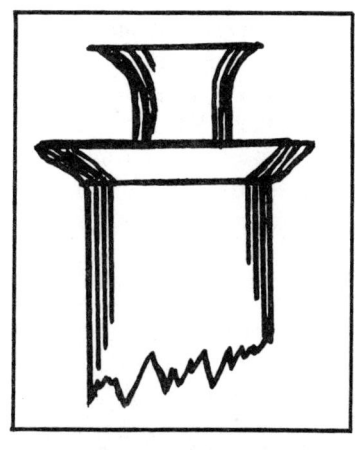

Fig. 5-14. The queen chess piece.

Add your name, address and telephone number inside. This is a good place to hold your fishing gear, collections and sewing supplies (Fig. 5-10).

ICE CANDLES

Take an empty 2 quart or 1 quart milk carton. Cut off the top of the box. Put a long wick anchored by a small piece of metal down in the bottom. Tie the upper end around a pencil and drop it over the top of the carton.

Pour melted paraffin (melt in a double boiler for safety) one-fourth full into the milk carton. Toss in cracked pieces of ice cubes (the odder the shapes, the more interesting the candle) on top of the hot paraffin.

Fig. 5-15. The bishop chess piece.

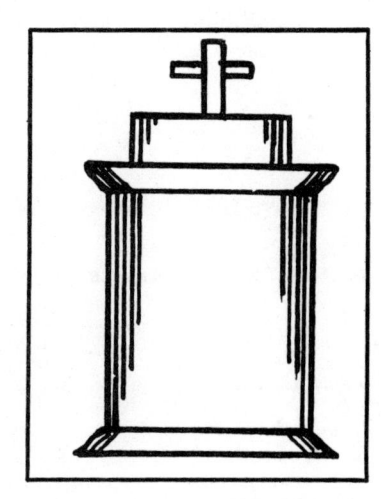

Pour the remainder of the paraffin as quickly as possible on top of the ice cubes up to the top of the carton. After the wax is hard, remove the paper carton and you will have a very unusual candle.

Here are extra tips for this type of candle. You can add scent and color to the paraffin. You can also stick a candle in the middle of the carton and drop paraffin and ice cubes around it, using it as a wick. In candle shops you can buy sheets of candle wax; however, it costs more (Fig. 5-11).

CLOTHESPIN CLIP

Use a spring type clothespin. From a piece of felt, cut out two small felt ears. Glue the bottom of them just before the metal piece on the clothespin. Glue two Indian seed beads eyes ahead of the ears.

Cut a small piece of red felt to make the mouth. Open the clothespin and glue the red mouth inside the top part of the clip.

If you want whiskers, use small pieces from the kitchen broom. Open the clip again and put a small bit of glue in the rounded cutout. Place the centers of the wool in the groove. Press into the glue and hold for a few minutes. Let it dry thoroughly (Fig. 5-12).

CHESSMEN FROM SPOOLS

Save your empty spools of thread. You will need four large ones, four medium ones and 16 small ones. Cut off the flange or leave it on as you desire.

Spray paint one-half of each of the sizes red and the other black. When paint is thoroughly dry, glue to one red and one black large spool a fancy gold top from a talcum box or perfume cap and crown from gold paper. These will be the kings (Fig. 5-13). For the queens, use a smaller top (Fig. 5-14). For the bishops, cut from

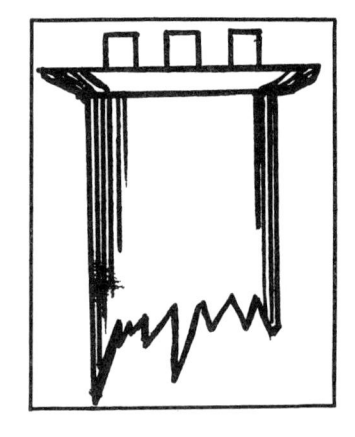

Fig. 5-16. The rook chess piece.

Fig. 5-17. The knight chess piece.   Fig. 5-18. The pawn chess piece.

heavy cardboard or balsa wood a ¼" cross and glue to the top (Fig. 5-15). For the rooks, you can cut heavy cardboard or the same balsa wood into ¼" squares and glue around the top to look like turrets of a castle (Fig. 5-16).

The knights will need a shield. This can be cut from cardboard that is about as wide as the spool and long enough to fit from under the top rim to the bottom. These may be designed as shown in Fig. 5-17 and painted two colors in opposite corners. For the pawns, use the spools with no decorations on them at all (Fig. 5-18).

ROBOT MARIONETTE

Use 1" styrofoam balls for the neck, arms and legs, 3" square for the head, 5" square for the body, two 2" squares for hands, two 2" × 3" rectangles for feet, and two 1" circles for ears. Use 1" circle for nose.

Use styrofoam glue and add ears to the head. Paint all balls, squares and rectangles silver, including the head. Use styrofoam paint. Paint the nose green and glue on. Paint a piece of styrofoam sheet, 3" × 2" and ¼" thick, and trace a pattern for the mouth. Cut out and glue in place. Add movable eyes (large).

Use green pipe cleaners for hair; stick in the head and crimp. Stick three green pipe cleaners in each hand, bending the front down to resemble stiff claws. Do the same with the feet, but do not let them bend lower than the bottom of the foot.

To assemble, use decorator's yarn long enough to string seven balls on with a knot between each ball, and enough left over the top and bottom to push and glue into both the feet and the bottom of the body. Glue these ends in.

Use another piece of yarn for each arm, long enough to string five balls with a knot in between each one and enough left over to glue into the hand and shoulder. Do the same with the neck, using three balls.

Paint two long straws silver and glue a small silver ball at the end of each. Glue in the head for the antenna (Fig. 5-19).

To make the control and string your marionette, use two pieces of slat wood crossed as shown in Fig. 5-20. Strings can be

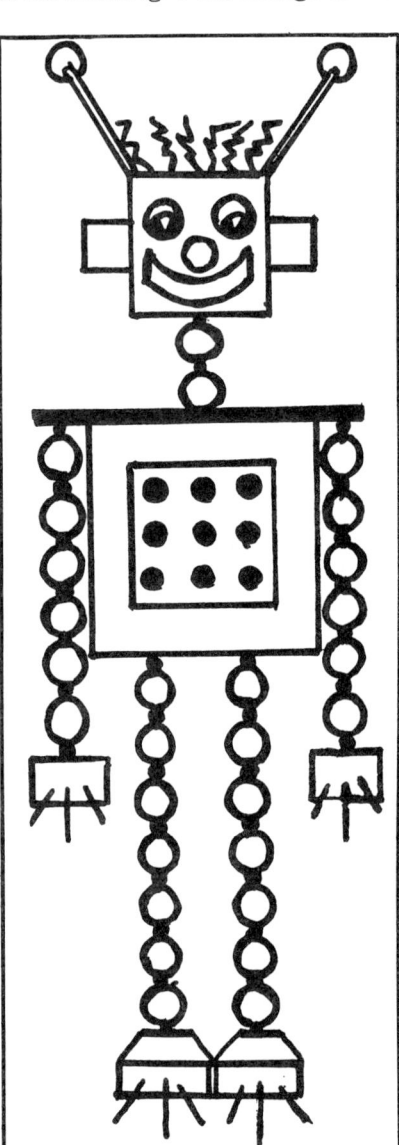

Fig. 5-19. Robot marionette.

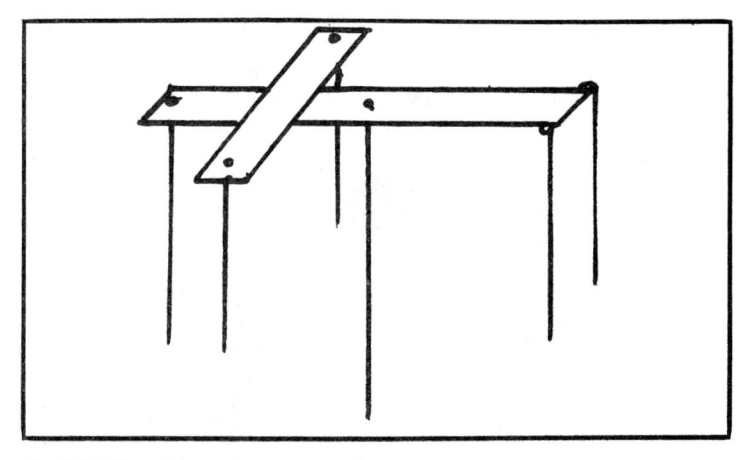

Fig. 5-20. The robot marionette control.

tied around the slats. Tie a string around the ends of the cross bar and attach to each foot. Tie two strings around the center strip and tie ends to each hand. Head strings are tied a little in back of that, and at the back tie one string and fasten it to the bottom of the robot's back. Make sure the strings are tied loosely enough so that his hands are straight down and his back is straight, until you pull them.

It will take a little while for you to learn how much manipulation you can do, so you will have to practice. By wiggling the control up and down, the robot will walk. Since he is a robot, it doesn't matter if the walk is stiff. Move the hands by pulling the strings that go to his hands by the hand that is not holding the control. If you bend the control downward, the robot will bow.

To complete the robot, you can add a panel of silver foil to his front. Paste glow colored circles on as though they were controls.

PAPER BAG PUPPETS

Choose a small, square-bottom lunch bag that is folded flat so that the square bottom of the lunch bag overlaps the front. Draw a funny face on the square bottom of the bag. Make sure it is in the middle so it will open and close. Add as many decorations to the bag as you wish.

You may draw an elephant, dog, cat or anything of your choice. Cut ears, nose, hair, etc, for the animal you create, using wool or felt. Glue them to the bag according to your design.

Fig. 5-21. Paper bag puppet.

Fig. 5-22. Paper bag Halloween mask.

Fig. 5-23. Pattern for a different nose for the paper bag Halloween mask.

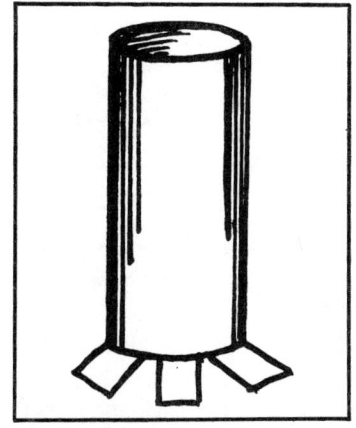

Fig. 5-24. Pattern for another nose for the paper bag Halloween mask.

Put your hand inside the bag so that your fingers will bend down into the square bottom. Open and close your hand. You can make your puppet speak and act (Fig. 5-21).

PAPER BAG HALLOWEEN MASKS

Place the bag over your head. While you have it on, make marks on it with a pencil where your eyes come and your nose and mouth touch. Take the bag off and draw the kind of eyes, nose and mouth you want. Make sure you make them much larger than your own for a mask is an exaggeration of features (Fig. 5-22).

If you wish to add a nose that sticks out, decide first the size and shape it will be before cutting out a place for it on your mask. There are a few in Figs. 5-23 and 5-24 for you to choose from.

After you have made the nose, place it on the face in the proper place. It should be right over your nose mark. Trace around the part that is to be pasted to the mask, and cut that area out. Insert the tabs and paste from the inside. Make sure they are colored first, so that they are easier to color.

Fig. 5-25. Pattern for ears for the paper bag Halloween mask.

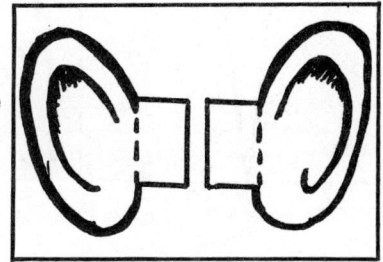

Fig. 5-26. Paper bag Halloween mask beak.

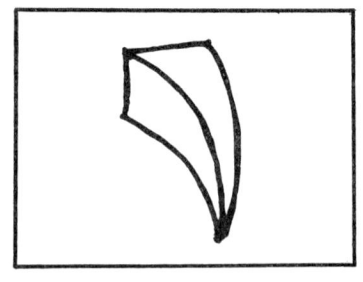

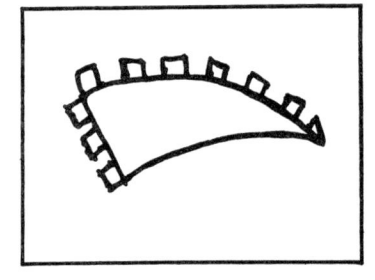

Fig. 5-27. Pattern for the sides of the beak.

Ears can be added by making slits in the side of the bag, inserting the tabs and pasting from the inside (Fig. 5-25). Hair can be added by using yarn pasted on top of the back and curled strips of papers. See Figs. 5-26 through 5-28.

EGG SHELL VASE

Take an ice pick and puncture a hole in either end of a raw egg. Blow out the contents and save for baking. Using the egg lengthwise, carefully cut off the top.

Take the egg shell and decorate it with bits of rickrack, felt, feathers, tiny buttons, lace and fur, sequins, seed beads or anything you may find in the sewing basket. You can make fancy hats and faces. Make the edges of the shells notched, or use a marker to outline the top of the egg. Color the eggs using a vegetable dye or leave them natural.

Glue some tiny pearls for legs on the bottom of the shell from an old strand of broken pearls, or use small buttons. They make nice favors for the dining table (Figs. 5-29 and 5-30).

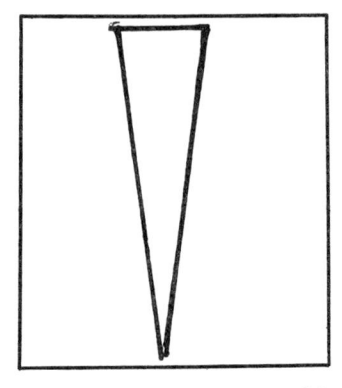

Fig. 5-28. Pattern for the top of the beak.

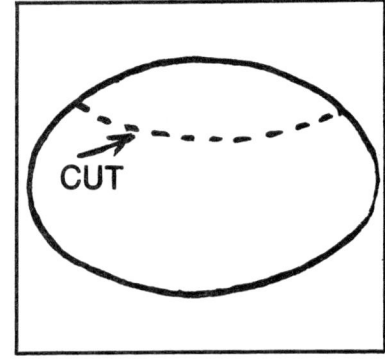

Fig. 5-29. Cutting pattern for the egg shell vase.

Fig. 5-30. A bouquet for the egg shell vase.

SPATTER PRINT BRIDGE TALLY CARD

Collect good specimens of leaves or ferns. Lay white paper down on the table. Lay a leaf on paper face down and cover with a fine mesh screening.

With a toothbrush, dip into a shallow container of green ink or wash bluing. Shake off excess liquid from brush. Stroke lightly over the outline of the leaf.

Carefully remove screening, and there will be a leaf print on the paper. This is a good idea for bridge tallies, notepaper, cards and favors (Fig. 5-31).

Fig. 5-31. Spatter print bridge tally card.

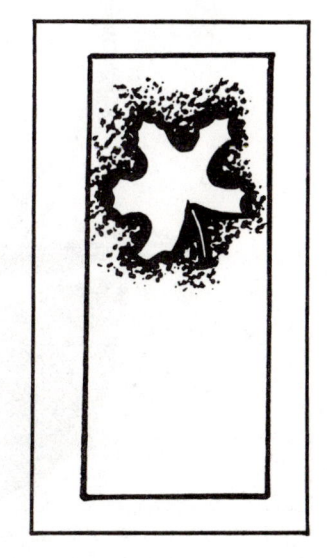

203

HANGING BASKET LETTUCE CRISPER

Use a lettuce crisper and weave ribbons in and out of the netting. Leave it plain and put a green hanging ivy plant in a pot, and then place it in the crisper (Fig. 5-32).

JAR PRETTIES

Use a baby jar, scrub well and dry. Paint the lid a flat black. When dry, decorate the glass with cutout flowers from a seed catalog or your own designs. If you are handy with the brush, paint on your own decorations. Jar pretties make good paper clip, pill, pin and catch-all jars (Fig. 5-33).

MARTIAN PAPERWEIGHTS

Find a couple of flat stones about 2½" for feet, a large oval stone about 4" for the body, and a medium sized oval stone about 2" for the head. Use epoxy cement and glue flat stones to the bottom of the body and an oval stone for the top of the head.

Fig. 5-32. Hanging basket flower holder from a lettuce crisper.

Fig. 5-33. A baby jar is used for the jar pretty.

Use fake fur for hair. Gather enough to form a circle, sew together and glue on top for the hair. Use movable eyes and glue in place. Add the top from a toothpaste or glue tube, painted red, for the nose. Paint on a mouth or use another cap.

Arms and hands may be painted on or made from cardboard and glued on in back. Paint feet black. Add pipe cleaner antenna and buttons or more caps (Fig. 5-34).

NAME PINS

Materials include round toothpicks or alphabet noodles and pins. Glue six to eight toothpicks on a small piece of cardboard. Paint or varnish.

Fig. 5-34. A Martian stone paperweight.

Fig. 5-35. A name pin from macaroni.

When dry, glue on letters of girls' or boys' names. Glue on a pin. A safety pin works well (Fig. 5-35).

CORN HUSK DOLLS

In the fall of the year, find some corn husks and dry them well. When you are ready to make the doll, douse the corn husks in a pail of water so they will be pliable.

Fig. 5-36. Corn husk doll.

Fig. 5-37. Apple doll.

Take a piece of corn husk and form a 2″ ball-shaped neck. Wrap a strong cord around the neck, leaving some corn husk dangling for the rest of the body.

Take another small wet corn husk and slip it in place crosswise under the neck to make the arms. Tie with a cord around the wrists and trim. Take another cord and tie the arms in place in the middle of the doll and around the waist. Glue corn silk on the head for hair. Pencil in the doll's face.

Take scraps from the work basket and create clothes for the corn husk doll or leave it natural.

Large corn husk dolls can be used as unusual Christmas tree ornaments and are often created for door swags or fall arrangements for the table (Fig. 5-36).

APPLE DOLLS

Choose a good winter apple that keeps well such as a Staymen, Winesap or McIntosh. Cut out the face with a paring knife. Dry the apple head for a few weeks in a dry place. Put the apple on a stick and dress according to the way you wish with scraps from Grandma's work basket (Fig. 5-37).

YARN DOLLIES

Use leftover balls of yarn. Cut a piece of cardboard 4" square. Wind yarn evenly and carefully around the 4" square about 30 times.

Then take two 4" strands of another color yarn and slip them under the yarn at the top of the cardboard. Tie the yarn well and slip out the cardboard. Cut the other end of the yarn at the opposite end of the knot.

To make the arms, wind the yarn around the 4" cardboard about 14 times. Slip out the cardboard and cut through each end of yarn. Tie the ends tightly at the wrists.

Now you will create the head. Tie the body about 1" down from the top. Divide the body in half and slip your arms up where they belong at the shoulders. Tie tightly at the waist with a knot.

Fig. 5-38. Yarn doll.

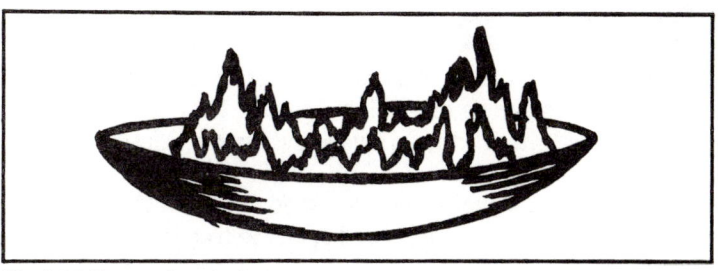

Fig. 5-39. Depression plant.

Take your scissors and trim the skirt evenly at the bottom of the doll. Use yarn of another color to sew on eyes, nose and mouth.

To make a boy yarn dolly, tie the skirt down. Divide the skirt and tie each end. This makes the trousers; trim evenly. Yarn dollies make good bookmarks, window hangs, tree decorations, package ties and toys for children (Fig. 5-38).

DEPRESSION PLANT OR CRYSTAL GARDEN

Mix the following:
- 4 tablespoons salt (not iodized)
- 4 tablespoons bluing
- 4 tablespoons water
- 1 tablespoon ammonia.

Pour this mixture over small bits of broken coal, brick or slag. Let stand for 24 hours.

If desired, take a medicine dropper and put a drop of vegetable color here and there on coal. The result resembles coral formation. You may use a milk glass or a clear or colored glass bowl for a container (Fig. 5-39).

Fig. 5-40. Japanese garden.

209

JAPANESE GARDEN

Choose a shallow dish. A rectangular type works well. Arrange colored chips or small pebbles in the bottom. Stick in pebbles, small bits of artificial foilage and tiny artificial flowers like straw flowers.

Find a small branch outside on a tree. Plant it into the pebbles as a tree, using small flowers tied upon the tree to represent the flowering cherry.

Add an oriental lady with a parasol and a small bridge in the center of the garden. You will find these articles in novelty or Japanese or Chinese stores.

For water, you may use a small mirror under the bridge. You may fill in around objects with some more foilage cut low and some larger, pretty stones. It makes a good conversation piece for the coffee table (Fig. 5-40).

SWEET POTATO GARDEN

Take a glass or pretty jar containing water. Place the sweet potato suspended by toothpicks so the end of the potato is covered with ½" of water. The toothpicks prevent the potato from rotting and hold it intact.

Place the garden in a sunny window, and in a few weeks pretty green vines will grow from the sweet potato. You can do this by cutting off the tops of carrots and turnips and laying them in saucers. They will sprout an attractive foilage (Fig. 5-41).

Fig. 5-41. Sweet potato garden.

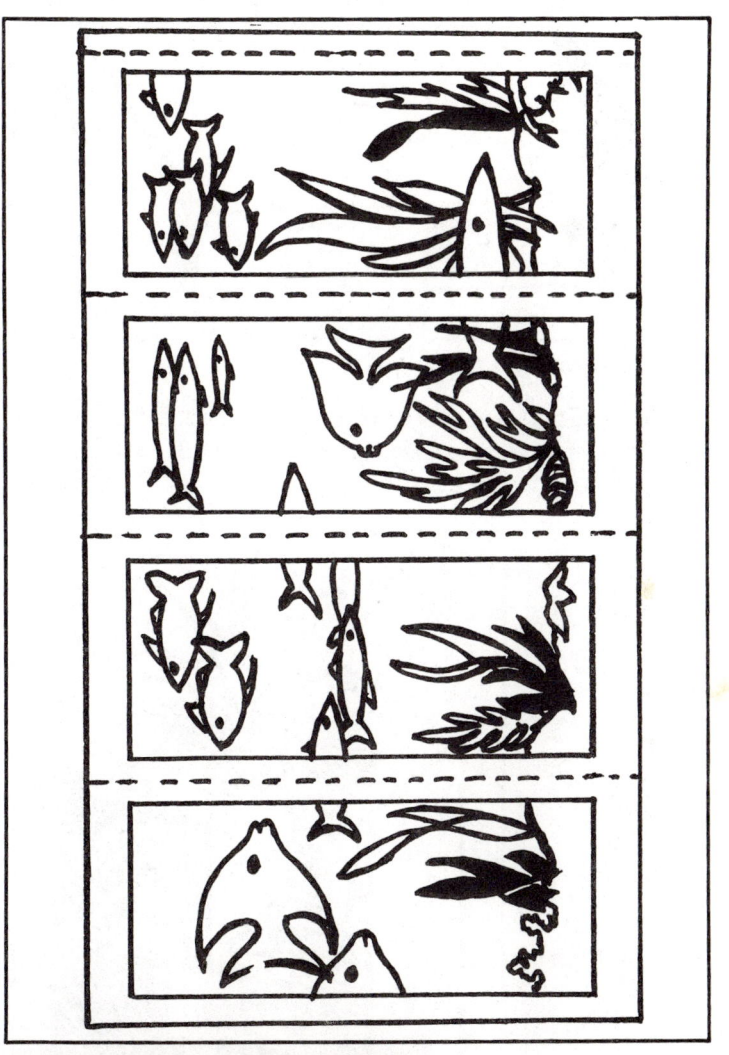

Fig. 5-42. An underwater scene candle cover.

UNDERWATER SCENE CANDLE COVER

    Cut from a piece of illustration board two pieces 20½" long × 12" high. Make a 1" margin at the top and bottom. Make a ½" margin on the left side and a 1" margin on the right side. Starting from the left ½" margin, measure off 4". Draw a line from the top to the bottom margin. From there, measure off two ½" marks and draw two lines from the top to the bottom. Repeat these measurements until you reach the end margin line.

211

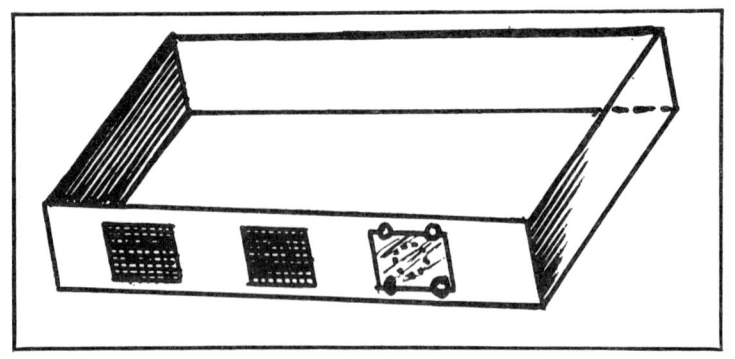

Fig. 5-43. Anthouse.

Score on both pieces of cardboard a line through the center of each of the three sections and in the middle of the 1″ section on the right. This will make it easier to fold.

Fig. 5-44. Memory box.

212

Fig. 5-45. An attractive bookplate.

Your inside section will be slightly smaller than the outer one when folded. You may have to cut the excess off the inner pattern at the ends. Make sure the candle itself is covered or use an "uncandle" so paper does not burn.

Get a piece of turquoise parchment paper that is 20″ × 11″. Paste this in back of the open areas. Fold the entire picture into four equal parts, gluing the left side ½″ margin underneath the right 1″ margin. Place over a candle in a holder. It will appear as

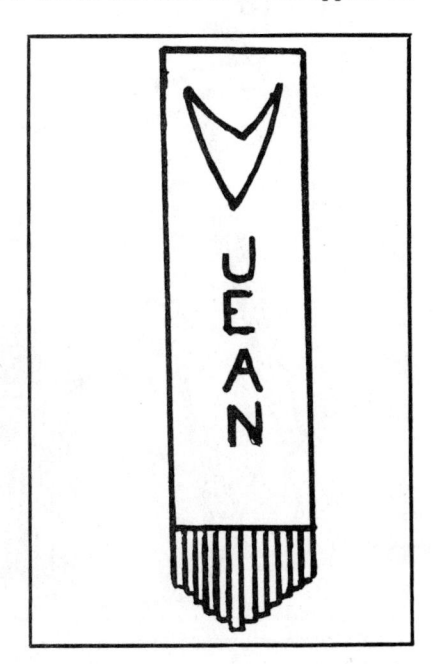

Fig. 5-46. A finished bookmarker.

though the colors of the water are changing as the candle shines (Fig. 5-42).

ANT HOUSE

Take four pieces of wood from the workbench or a lumber mill, 6" to 7" long and 2" wide. This will make the shallow rectangular frame for the house.

Nail edges together. Then cut out three holes, and measure 1½" wide on one side of the frame.

Use a piece of fine wire screening. Cover and tack this over two of the ventilating holes. Using the third hole, tack a piece of lightweight tin over the hole. Be sure the tin is slightly larger than the hole opening. Nail your tacks above and below the tin so the door may be moved from side to side. Through this little door you will feed the ants.

Find two pieces of window glass that will fit the top and bottom of the frame. Fasten glass to the frame with a heavy tape.

Now you are ready to find an ant community that will move into your new ant house. You will find an ant colony under a log, a

Fig. 5-47. Iron-on patches for the apron.

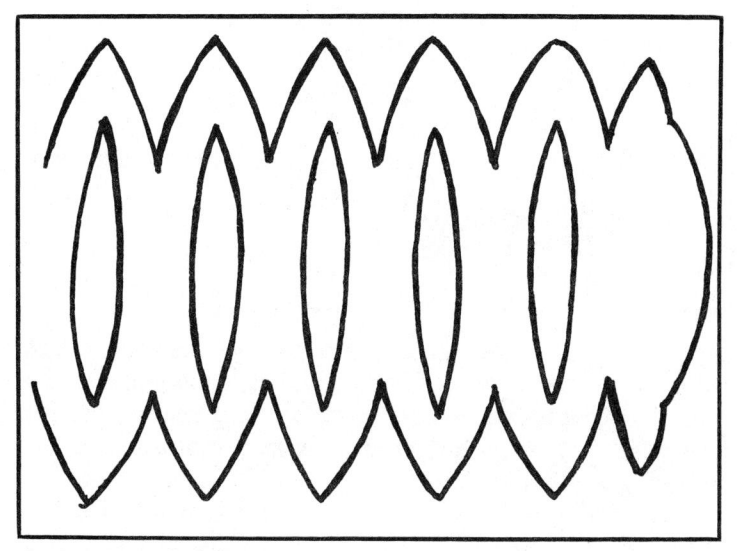

Fig. 5-48. Leather belt.

large stone or near an old tree stump. With a shovel, carefully dig some earth from under the anthill, trying not to disturb the colony. You will see some whitish eggs. Try to collect about 60 worker ants. These are the ants that are busily running in and out of the entrace to the anthill. When you get home, open up the bag carefully and push ants through the little door using a small fruit spoon, tweezers or a cardboard scoop. Try not to injure them.

To care for the ants, feed them every day with a small bit of honey placed on a cookie, a sugar lump soaked in water, cake crumbs or any sweet dampened tidbit. Always have a small jar lid full of water at all times in the house. You can keep the ant house moist by squirting water over it with an eye dropper through the little tin door. Never place the ant house in full sun.

Sit back and watch the ant community work. They will keep you entertained with their interesting busy life. If you tire of this project, take the ant house out to the woods and release the ants so they can take up their work (Fig. 5-43).

MEMORY BOX

Find an old antique picture frame at a garage sale or shop. Remove the back of the frame.

Build an extension to the frame to make the shadow box. Take pieces of wood about ½" thick × 3" wide. Measure the length and width of the frame and use these measurements for extension. Nail

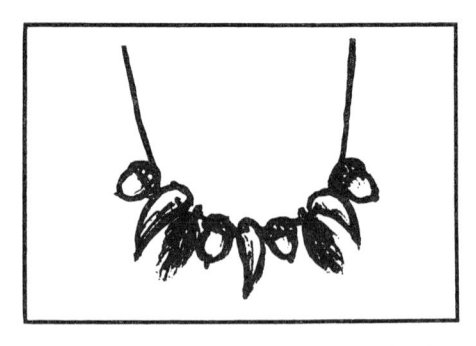

Fig. 5-49. African necklace.

them together and attach them to the frame's open back. Be sure to close the back with wood. Divide the front of the frame on the inside into compartments using ½" thick wood. Sand and varnish new wood that has been added or paint a contrasting color, depending on your picture frame.

You can either create a memory box of your childhood or married life. If it is patterned after your childhood, find a good picture of your parents and glue it in the middle compartment. In the other sections, put miniature articles of your talents that makes you a special person. If you are a writer, add a small book or a little pen; if you like handcraft, add a small clam shell with some bread dough flowers; if you enjoy nature, add a miniature bird nest and ceramic bird. Use your personal Sunday School pins or ribbons you have saved as a child, your scout or campfire pins, ets. For your married life, use the pictures of your children and articles that mean something to you personally.

When every article has been glued or hung with a hook in the memory box, glass it in so it will be safe. These make wonderful family gifts—meaningful, unusual and inexpensive (Fig. 5-44).

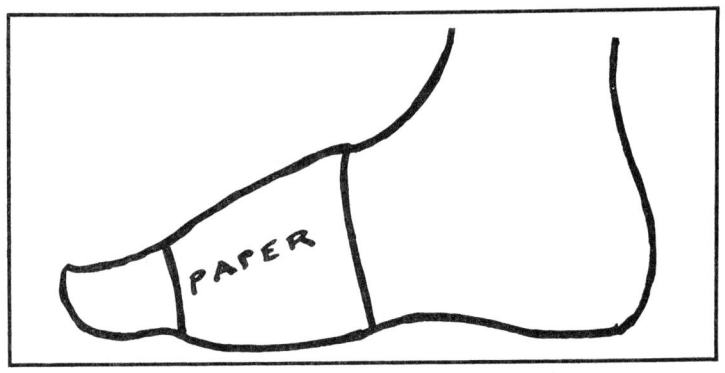

Fig. 5-50. Place a piece of paper around your foot.

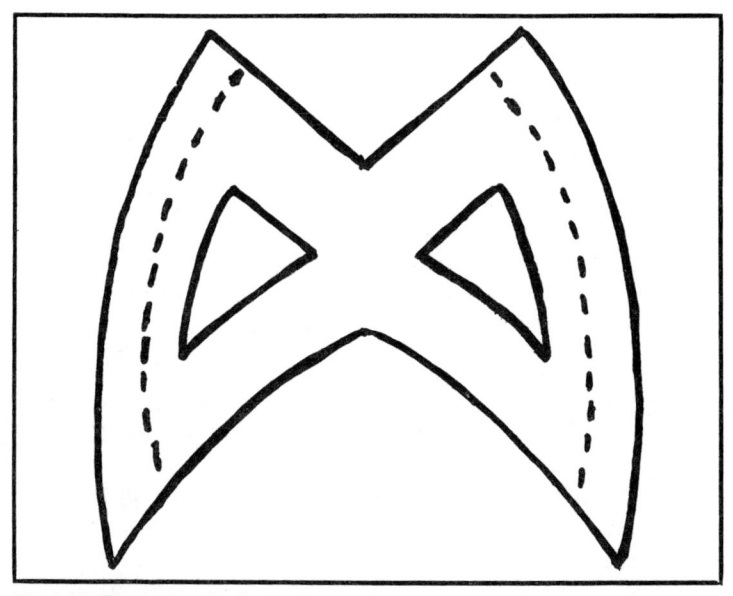

Fig. 5-51. Toe pattern for the leather scuffs.

BOOKPLATE

Take a pencil and lightly mark a piece of gummed paper or plain paper. Use a piece of heavy tracing paper. With your ruler and pencil, draw a few 2½" × 3" rectangles. Write or print your name neatly. Draw a pretty design on the bookplate with a border around the edge.

Now take your traced design and turn it over. Take a soft pencil and hold it horizontally, using the side of the pencil tip. Run your pencil back and forth over the tracing paper until the back of your design is all black.

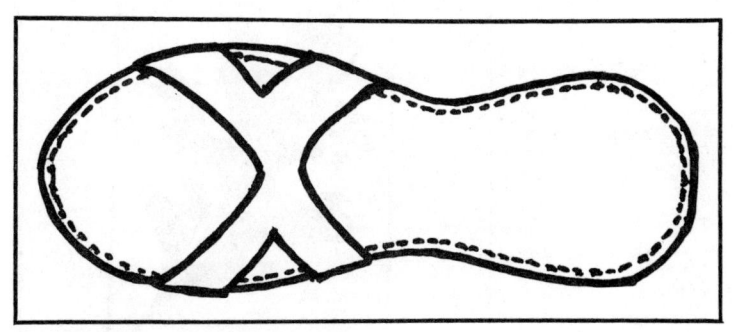

Fig. 5-52. The completed leather scuffs.

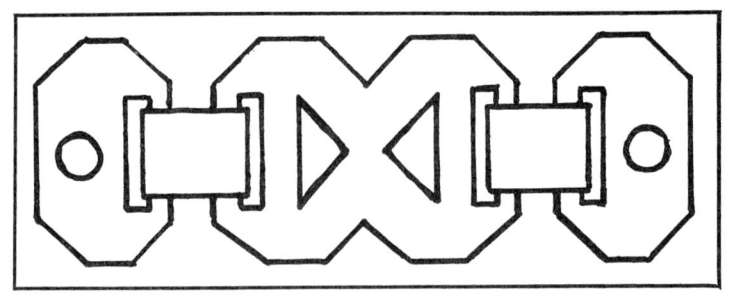

Fig. 5-53. Plastic link belt.

Put your traced bookplate paper on top of your gummed paper, with the stick side down, making sure your rectangular borders will match. Take your pencil and retrace your design. This transfers your design to the gummed paper.

Continue doing this until you have used all of your bookplates. Then take a pen and go over your pencil design to make it stand out. You are ready to cut out your bookplates. When they are cut, they personalize the books in your library (Fig. 5-45).

BOOKMARKER

Enlarge the pattern and trace onto medium weight leather. Cut out the triangular part of the top. The tab will slip over the page. Fringe the bottom (Fig. 5-46).

PATCH FUN

Purchase some colored iron-on patches. Take a pencil and trace one of your favorite designs on the patch. Examples are flowers, mushrooms, initials, leaves, etc.

Fig. 5-54. Smoke print.

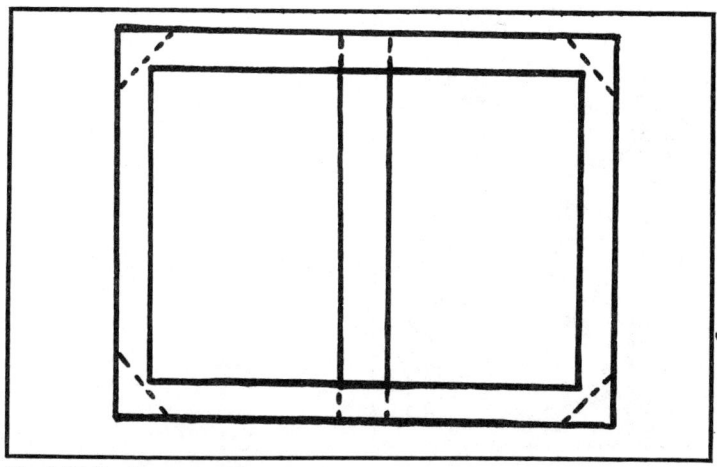

Fig. 5-55. Book cover pattern.

Take scissors and cut around the design. Place it on your sweatshirt, jeans or apron that you wish to decorate. Heat up the iron and iron on the patch (Fig. 5-47).

LEATHER BELT

Figure 5-48 is only one portion of the belt, showing the end that will slip into the last opening to hold the belt closed. Measure your waist and trace as many sections as you will need to go around your waist, but trace only one of the closing section.

Cut out with a sharp knife. You can stain leather or merely give it a good polish with a clear leather polish.

Fig. 5-56. Method of decorating the book cover.

219

Fig. 5-57. The completed book cover.

AFRICAN NECKLACE

Use nuts, seeds and feathers for your necklace. Dry out the nuts and seeds and drill small holes through them so they can be strung. You will have to use a good glue. Glue a small loop of cord at the end of the feathers in order to string it. Alternate large nuts, seeds and feathers. String on a cord. They can be painted if you wish (Fig. 5-49).

SCUFFS

Place both of your feet on a piece of brown wrapping paper, and trace around them to get the size of the soles. Since these

Fig. 5-58. A hair clip can be used for a page clip.

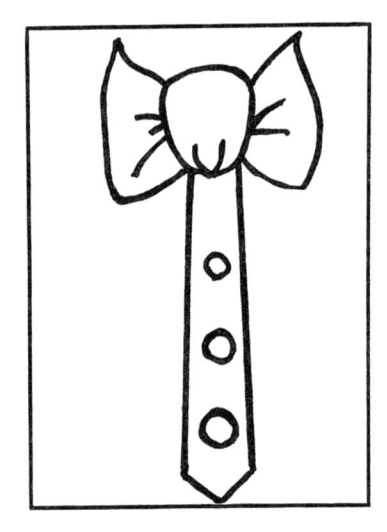

220

Fig. 5-59. Flower stationery.

scuffs are not for outside wear, you do not have to use a heavy sole leather. A medium weight will do. You will, however, need a thinner weight leather for the inner sole and the upper section.

Trace your pattern for the soles on both the heavier weight and lighter weight leather that you are using for the insoles and cut out. Take a piece of thin paper, such as typewriter paper. Place it on top of your foot, allowing it to go underneath your feet. See Fig. 5-50. Trace around the side of the foot and remove. This will give you the shape you will need to go over your instep, but you will need to add ½" to the sides to cement to the soles.

Fig. 5-60. Example of a valentine card.

Fig. 5-61. A valentine card with two hearts intertwined.

After removing the paper, cut the front and back portion of the top piece according to the pattern. Lay on a piece of the lighter weight leather and cut out.

When all pieces are cut out, cement the inner sole to the bottom, inserting the upper portion of the scuff ½" between the two soles and in the proper position. Try the scuff on before sewing to make sure you do not have to make any adjustments.

With a leather punch and using the smallest hole, punch holes through both pieces of leather and the three pieces inside where the upper portion is. Place holes ¼" in from the edge and ¼" apart. Lace the shoe together with a stitching awl and heavy linen thread used for that purpose. (Figs. 5-51 and 5-52).

LINK BELT

The belt may be made from leather or plastic oleo lids. For the designed part of the belt, use scrap sole leather that you can get from any leather factory. You will need to get thin leather for links and gimp for tying.

Trace the design onto the heavy leather with carbon paper. With a sharp knife, cut out white areas. Links will be about 1¼" long so you can figure how many designs and links you will need to go around your waist. Leave about 1" or 1½" open in front for the tie.

Cut out all links and designs. Assemble the belt by linking through two designs and riveting in back. When all are linked

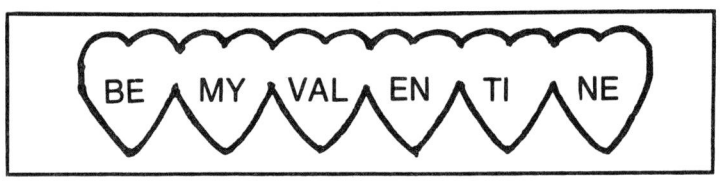

Fig. 5-62. A folding valentine card.

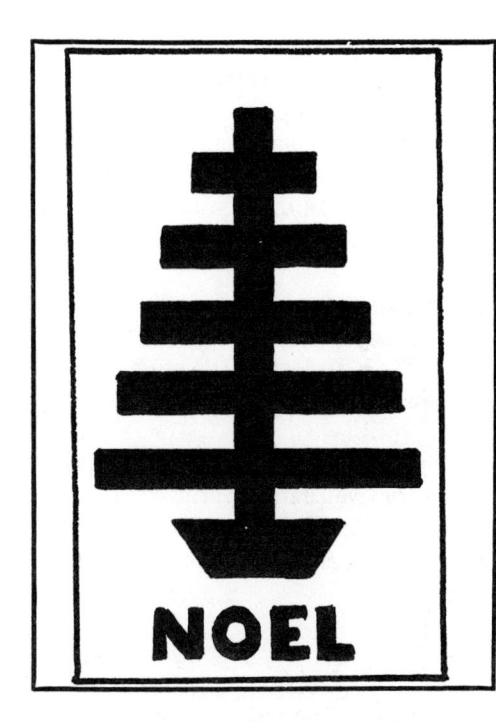

Fig. 5-63. The "noel" Christmas card.

together, take about 36" of gimp and fold in half. Each link is cut the same except the one that holds the links together. The plain strip is stapled in the back. It holds the two strips together.

On the last two designed links, do not cut an opening for a link at one end. Punch a hole instead.

For the plastic belt, trace the design from the book onto lightweight cardboard and cut out. Tape this to the underside of a piece of plastic can lid. With a sharp took, trace the design onto plastic. Cut out. Use the same kind of plastic for links. The procedure for linking the belt together is the same as above, but links can be stapled together in the back. These plastic ones may be colored with permanent marking pens if you like. For the tie on the plastic belt, use heavy silk cord (Fig. 5-53).

SMOKE PRINTING

Use an empty pop bottle and coat it with some kind of grease like lard or vaseline. Fill the bottle with cold water and cork tightly.

Collect some leaves you would like to preserve. Take a candle and light the wick. Hold the bottle sideways over the flame until it is black. It must be large enough to cover your leaf specimen.

Put the leaf, vein side up, on a piece of newspaper. Roll up the blackened part of the bottle over the leaf. Remove your leaf from the newspaper pad and lay it vein side up on clean newspaper.

Cover the leaf with a clean sheet of plain white paper. Roll a clean soda pop bottle over the white sheet. This will make the print on your paper. Another method (use caution) of smoke printing is to lightly grease a white sheet of paper with lard or some shortening.

Carefully turn the greased side over a lighted candle and move quickly until the paper is black. Lay it down on the table with the blackened part facing upward. Place the leaf face down on smoked paper, cover with a piece of newspaper and rub thoroughly until the leaf is smoked.

Carefully place the leaf on a fresh white piece of paper. Cover with another piece of paper and rub well until the print comes off of the leaf onto paper. Remove the leaf and cover the paper. Be careful of grease spots on finished paper. Smoke prints are nice for decorating notepaper (Fig. 5-54).

BOOK COVER

Lay out the book you wish to cover as flat as possible and trace the size onto brown wrapping paper. Add 1½" to all sides. Trace

Fig. 5-64. A Christmas card showing holly and pine needles.

Fig. 5-65. A Christmas card depicting Santa Claus.

the pattern on white wrapping paper and lay under the book (Fig. 5-55). Draw lines from the outside of the pattern where the back is to the book, and cut those two pieces out. Draw a triangle at each corner about ¼" from edge of book. Cut off the corners.

Use a metal pan long enough to be able to lay the paper onto it. Fill the pan with at least 1" of water (Fig. 5-56). Drop several colors of enamel onto the top of the water and swirl around with a stick. Roll paper across the water, and it will pick up the swirled design. Allow the paper to thoroughly dry.

When the paper is dry, lay it on the book, fold over the edges and close the book. This will show you where you must glue or tape the cover on the book so that it will not bind (Fig. 5-57).

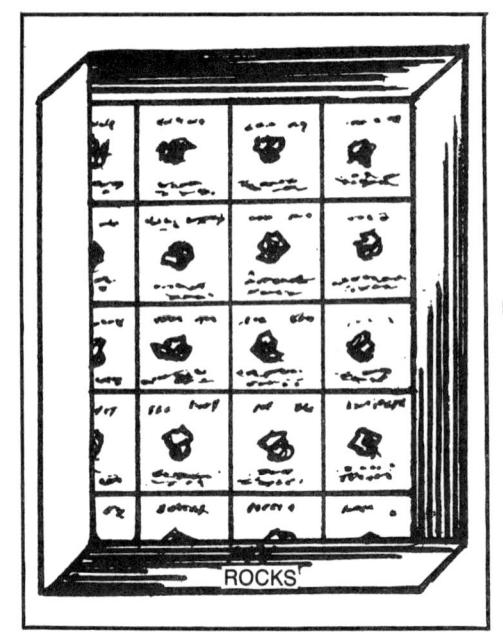

Fig. 5-66. Rock collection.

HAIR CLIP FOR A PAGE CLIP

Glue the complete top of a hair clip. Set on top a felt design you have drawn and cut out with scissors. Designs might be a narrow leaf, a pear, a feather or a necktie.

Decorate the felt according to the design used. The use of different colored pieces of felt makes it attractive.

Do the same for the back side of the clip when the front is completely dried. Then put the clip to work by clipping onto the page of your book (Fig. 5-58).

Fig. 5-67. The bird nest garden.

Fig. 5-68. A "quiet" sign.

Fig. 5-69. A "private" sign.

NATURE CREATIONS ON NOTEPAPER

You will need the following materials:
- Pressed dried flower, leaves, etc. from woods and fields.
- A sheet of cardboard approximately 11" × 14".
- Thumbtacks or masking tape.
- A varnish brush 1½" wide.
- Plastic waxed paper in sheets or rolls.
- Elmer's glue thinned with water 1 to 4 parts.
- Scott tissue, white and tinted, of wet strength.
- Glitter in assorted colors if desired.
- Envelopes and matching notepaper. Note that the size of the envelope determines the final design dimension.
- Scalloping or pinking shears for cutting the border.

Mark an approximate 8 × 5 border on cardboard as shown (Fig. 5-59). This may vary according to envelope size. Lay a sheet of waxed paper over the border area. Fasten down the corners with tape or thumbtacks.

Spread thinned glue with a brush over the design area. Apply tissue over the design and smooth out wrinkles. Sprinkle on glitter over the area if desired.

When dry, press with a low heat iron. Fold in half with inserted notepaper. Trim with shears to fit a matching envelope.

VALENTINE CARDS

The card in Fig. 5-60 is made from white paper about 6" × 9" folded to make a long triangle, 4½" × 6". Fold a piece of red paper

Fig. 5-70. A "keep out" sign.

Fig. 5-71. A "do not distrub" sign.

Fig. 5-72. A plastic key holder with initials.

3½″ × 4½″ in half to make a heart. Fold a still smaller piece of pink paper in half to make a heart for the center. Cut a strip of white crepe paper long enough to go around the large heart and about ½″ wide.

Paste crepe paper around the edge of the large red heart, crinkling the edges or ruffling them. Paste the pink heart on top of the red one only around the edges. In the center of the pink heart draw a door. Cut across the top of the door and bottom and through

Fig. 5-73. A plastic key holder with a name.

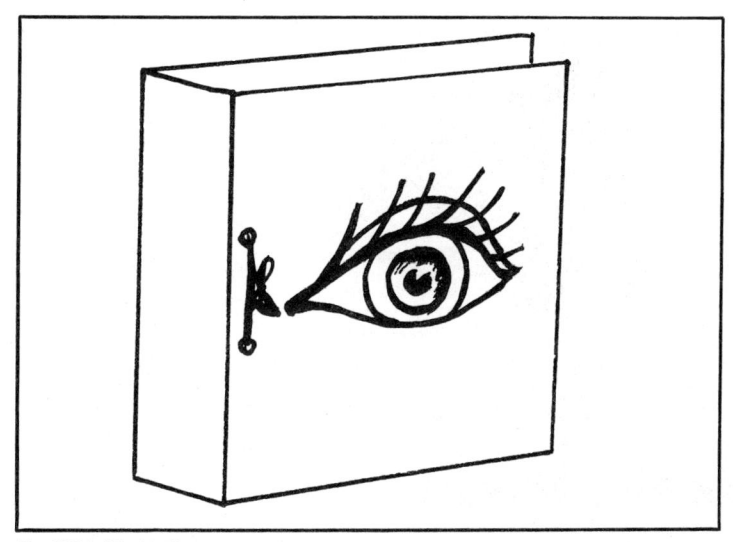

Fig. 5-74. Photo album cover.

the center of both the pink and red paper underneath, so that it can be folded back like a door. Paste the completed heart on pink paper. Open the door and paste a piece of white paper to fit inside. Print on that, "I love you."

The card in Fig. 5-61 is made of white paper folded so that it is longer than tall. Fold red paper to make a heart and trace so the other is the same size. Paste hearts as indicated in Fig. 5-61. With a ruler, draw a line to indicate the arrow. Make slits in the top sheet where marked. Use a dental applicator cut to fit the card and insert through the slits, allowing it to stick out both ends. Cut a gold arrow point from gold metallic paper and glue over one end. The feather end can be made from thin strips of gold paper or a real feather.

The card in Fig. 5-62 is made from a piece of white paper 12" × 3". Fold the card at every 2", each one in back of the other. Draw a red heart 3" wide × 2" long and paste one on each fold of white, so

Fig. 5-75. Scrub a clam shell and let it dry.

229

Fig. 5-76. Clam shell garden flower arrangement.

that when it is opened it will be a line of six red hearts. Using a black marking pen, print on each heart as indicated in Fig. 5-62. Fold to send.

EASY CHRISTMAS CARDS

Fold white paper in half, making cards wider than long or longer than wide. For the card in Fig. 5-63, cut strips of green paper and paste on the card as illustrated. Use a bright red for the pot. If you prefer, you can use ribbon for stripes and wide braid to cut a pot. Print "noel" with white crayon or paint.

The card in Fig. 5-64 has a white background, too. Holly and evergreen are made with a marking pen. Paint or use marking pens to make stems. Cut out holly berries from glossy red paper and paste over the holly. Use single strips of red ribbon to simulate the bow and use a red marking pen to write "hello."

The card in Fig. 5-65 also has a white background, but unlike the others it is made by pasting colored paper over the white. Cut a

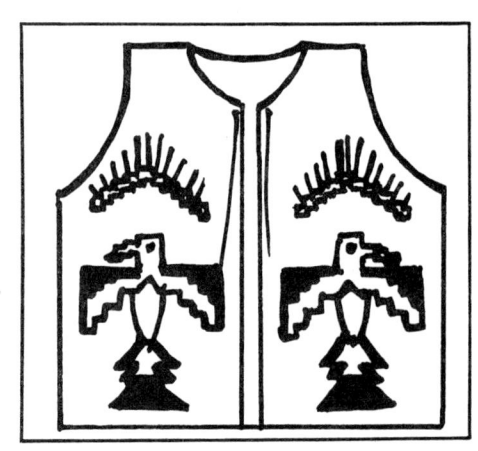

Fig. 5-77. Suede cloth vest.

Fig. 5-78. Shoe shine mitt.

long piece of pink paper for the face and paste a little below the middle of the card. Cut a small red circle and glue in the center for nose. Cut two white circles and paste above for the eyes, adding a dot of blue in the center of each. Fold a strip of white paper in half, draw half of a mustache and cut out. Glue under the nose.

The beard is made of small strips of white paper curled at one end and pasted as shown (Fig. 5-65). Add a small, red oval mouth. The hat is made of two red triangles. One is pasted above the face to allow for a white rim at the bottom of the hat. The other is pasted to follow the line of the left side of the hat and to stick out on the

Fig. 5-79. Carry-all bag.

Fig. 5-80. The jar is filled with seashells.

right side hanging down. Add the white strip across the bottom of the hat and the round piece for the ball at the bottom of the hat.

ROCK COLLECTION

Secure an empty egg carton. Carry with you a drawstring bag to hold pebbles and rocks that you collect. You will find them in the brook, along a road or in the woods—almost anywhere.

Get an identification rock book from the library or purchase a paperback one. On the inside cover, print the key position of each rock you identify. Using the egg carton, place a specimen into each compartment and label. You can also mount your specimens on heavy cardboard using glue and wire or heavy string to hold them to the board (Fig. 5-66).

SEWING CARDS

Cut out a picture from a magazine of an animal, machine or fruit. Glue it on a piece of cardboard. Trim the picture evenly so it will match the cardboard.

Fig. 5-81. Shell centerpiece.

Fig. 5-82. Broomstick skirt.

Allow the picture to dry well. Take a paper hole puncher and punch holes around the outline of the picture.

Use heavy yarn with a large eyed embroidery needle to sew through the punched holes, following the outline of the picture. Children will love sewing cards on a rainy day.

BIRD NEST GARDEN

During the winter season, find a bird's nest in the crotch of a tree. Never collect the nest during the nesting season.

Place the empty bird nest in a saucer or water in your house on a sunny window sill. A garden will grow from the nest in a few weeks from all the small seeds interwoven in the nest. Be sure to keep the nest damp (Fig. 5-67).

CUTOUT SIGNS

You can get your message across to your family and friends by making these colorful signs for your door. All you need is a small piece of cardboard. Even stiff paper will do, about 4" × 6" or 6" × 12", depending on what you have to say. Find different colored letters of different types to spell out your words from magazines. The more diverse the letters are, the better it will look. Cut them out and paste them on the background in a haphazard way, not in a straight line. Put two holes at the top to hang on your door (Figs. 5-68 through 5-71).

KEY HOLDERS

Use plastic lids for these and clean off any printing with a cleansing powder. The designs in Figs. 5-72 and 5-73 are merely suggestions. You can make up your own design.

Fig. 5-83. Needle holder.

Draw the design on paper first and trace it onto the plastic with heavy carbon paper. A sharp tool can be used if you can sew through the plastic. If you can see through it you tape the design underneath the lid and use the sharp tool to trace. Color with permanent ink marking pens or nail polish.

PHOTO ALBUM COVER

Decide on the size you want for your book and about how thick it should be to hold your photos. You can use the lids from gift boxes or even cartons for this project.

Cut three pieces of your cardboard that are wider than deep, such as 15" × 10" or thereabouts. Cut another piece that is the same depth as the cover and about 3" wide for the end. About 2" in from each side of the cover, front and back, draw a line down the depth of the cover and score the cardboard. (See the chapter on special techniques.) This will enable you to open the album easier.

You can cover the cardboard by painting it or by using contact paper. If you use contact paper, lay the cardboard out flat on the paper before you cut. Allow at least 1" or more at the top, bottom

Fig. 5-84. The walnut shell turtle.

Fig. 5-85. A sock doll.

and sides for turning over. Cut out the contact paper and adhere, turning the ends over as you would for any book cover.

In the middle of the side of the book, where you allowed 2" before you scored it, punch two holes about 3" apart. This is where you will hold your book together.

You can use heavy packaging wool or twine for the tie. Make the inside pages of a neutral color or black construction paper. Make sure you put the holes in the same place. Fill the book and tie in front.

Fig. 5-86. The rag book is a nice gift for young children.

235

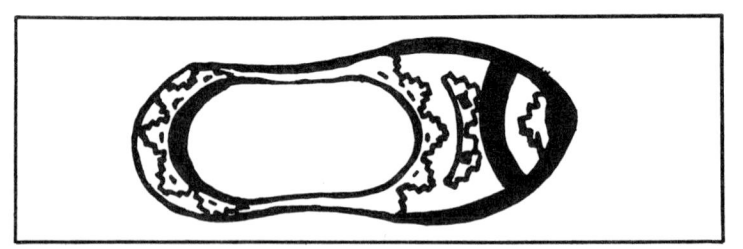

Fig. 5-87. Top view of the beaded moccasin.

If you wish to make a lining for the cover other than the same paper you used for the outside, cut it about ½" smaller than the outside measurement of the book. Paste it on (Fig. 5-74).

CLAM SHELL GARDEN

Scrub and clean a clam shell and let it dry well. Fill it with clay and arrange small artificial flowers or tiny straw flowers with foilage in the center (Figs. 5-75 and 5-76).

SUEDE CLOTH VEST

Purchase 1¼ yards of suede cloth and 5 yards of binding for piping. If you do not have a pattern for a vest, take an old blouse and cut out the sleeves. Do not cut the vest as full as the blouse. You want the vest to be straight up and down.

Draw Indian designs on a piece of scrap paper. You will find Indian designs and symbols in the library in an Indian book. Trace the designs onto bright, solid colored fabric. Take the cutouts, pin on the vest front and hand sew with small stitches. You can also use an ornamental stitch on your sewing machine. Sew piping around edges of the vest. Attach at the neck with a leather thong sewed to each side. Use a bootlace (Fig. 5-77).

SHOE SHINE MITT

Take two pieces of felt and cut with the pinking shears into the shape of a mitten. Sew together on the sewing machine or by hand. If sewing by hand, you can sew a running or feather stitch in another

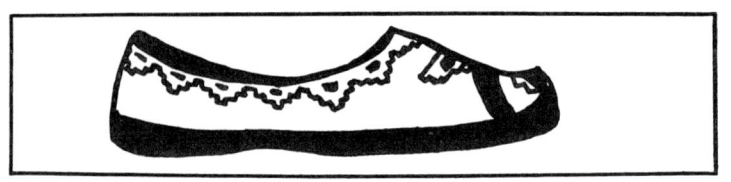

Fig. 5-88. Side view of the beaded moccasin.

Fig. 5-89. Felt change purse.

color to make it attractive. Draw a design of a shoe (using a magic marker) on the top and embroider with a bright color (Fig. 5-78).

CARRY-ALL BAG

Visit a discount store and purchase a heavy piece of canvas, at least ½ yard. Cut a square 12 × 12. Sew up three sides (on the wrong side) with heavy thread, leaving the top open. Turn down and hem 1" wide.

If the fabric is plain, decorate it with appliqué designs or your initials. Cut two pieces of material 2" wide and 18" long. Stitch the handles to the sides of the canvas bag. One of these bags will outlast a store-bought one (Fig. 5-79).

Fig. 5-90. Felt pencil case.

COLLECTION OF SEASHELLS

If you have an antique half gallon jar with a handle and lid, you have a special place to exhibit your collection of seashells. Fill the jar full of shells, placing them in an attractive manner. Use a dried sea horse for novelty. You will hear your guests comment on the unique way you have displayed your collection. The old mason quart jar may be used with a zinc lid (Fig. 5-80).

SHELL DECOR

If you are fortunate enough to have a huge conch type shell, bore a hole carefully through the top of the shell. Fill the bowl of the shell with an artificial arrangement. Change with the seasons and hang in your window. The big shell may also be placed on floristic clay using a low plate for the base. Fill the shell with live plants, watering once a week (Fig. 5-81).

BILL COLLECTOR

Find an old ice pick with a wooden handle. Drill a hole in a 4" board, ½" thick, to hold the wooden end of the ice pick handle. Glue the wooden end of the pick into the hole. Varnish the block of wood and the handle of the ice pick. The point of the ice pick will keep your bills from straying.

BROOMSTICK SKIRT

Purchase 1 or 2 yards of brightly printed fabric (according to your size). Sew it into a skirt gathered to a band. Soak it well in water until the fabric is dripping wet.

In its dripping condition, take an old broomstick and fold the skirt as tight as you can around the stick. Tie it securely and hang it in the sun to dry.

When dry, unroll and try the skirt on. This is an old method of creating a fancy skirt (Fig. 5-82).

Fig. 5-91. Flower pot base.

Fig. 5-92. Antique china piece plant holder.

NEEDLE HOLDER

Trace a design of a little lady with a sun bonnet from a nursery rhyme book onto a piece of paper and cut it out. Lay it on a piece of felt and cut it out with the pinking shears. Embroider fancy designs like little flowers on her dress, and outline her bonnet with embroidery floss.

On the inside of the skirt, add another piece of felt to hold the needles. The inner skirt should be shorter than the outer skirt. Stitch the inner skirt to the outer skirt at the waist (Fig. 5-83).

WALNUT SHELL TURTLE

Take one-half of a walnut shell and place it down on the table in front of you. Glue little shields from a pine cone for legs, two in the front and two in the back. Paint eyes of white on the lower part of the head. Glue a little shield to stick out under the shell at the head for the mouth (Fig. 5-84).

SOCK DOLLS

Buy a pair of men's work socks. Cut off the toe and save pieces. The heel of the sock is the back of the doll.

Cut up at the toe 2" high. These will be divided off for the legs. Stuff the sock as full as possible with foam or cotton.

Sew the toe pieces in a trianglular shape and stuff them, stitching them to the front of the sock. Turn down the top of the sock and stitch together with heavy thread.

On the front of the sock, embroider the face with floss or sew buttons on for the eyes and embroider the rest of the face. Tie at the neck with a tight cord. A baby's sock done in this manner makes the nicest gift (Fig. 5-85).

RAG BOOK

Cut pieces of material 10" × 10". Use pinking shears to trim pages which are cut smaller. Fasten the pages together with shoestring drawn through punched holes in the sides of pages.

For the cover, use a heavy piece of upholstery material. Gather together bright colored pictures from magazines and glue to the pages of the book. When completed, fasten them together. Glue a big picture on the cover of some animal or toy. This is a great gift for younger children who enjoy books (Fig. 5-86).

MOCCASIN DECORATING

Purchase in a store a soft pair of suede shoes or leather moccasins. Draw a design on the top of the moccasin.

Buy some Indian seed beads in a craft shop. With a strong nylon thread, sew on the beads following the line of the design. Use the Indian strong colors: green, orange, blue, yellow, black, white, red and brown (Figs. 5-87 and 5-88).

FELT CHANGE PURSE

Cut with pinking shears a piece of felt 3 × 5. Use one piece of felt that is 5" for the back part of the purse so you will have a 2" flap to turn over.

Stitch them together on a sewing machine, or you can use an ornamental stitch in yarn. Let the top open and turn the flap over the front. Sew a snap on the flap to keep the purse closed, or use magnetic tape (Fig. 5-89).

FELT PENCIL CASE

Measure pencils and cut two pieces of felt long enough to fit the pencils. Make one piece longer than the other to form a flap. Stitch them together with the sewing machine or overcast the sides with embroidery floss or yarn (Fig. 5-90).

FLOWERPOT BASE

Take one of your favorite potted house plants and glue four tiles around a flower pot, gluing end to end. For a firm base, glue on one for the bottom, attaching it to the four sides. You can often find tiles on the bargain counters in stores (Fig. 5-91).

ANTIQUE CHINA PIECE PLANT HOLDER

If you have some lovely antique china pieces without tops (or maybe they have a crack), use them to make a lovely plant holder. Place drainage pebbles or gravel in the bottom and fill the pitcher bowl, gravy boat or sugar bowl with good brown garden soil.

Plant a *Wandering Jew,* miniature ivy or any small leaved trailing plant into the container. Water once a week by sinking the container into water that just flows above the rim until bubbles stop bubbling. Stand on a corner of the mantel or high shelf so that the plant can trail (Fig. 5-92).

AUTOGRAPH DACHSHUND

Find a paper towel cardboard tube and cover it with brown wrapping paper, or cut some from a paper bag. For the head, use an egg-shaped styrofoam ball. Paint it brown and attach to the body with glue, or use a corsage-pin. Use movable eyes and a piece of red felt for the mouth and glue on two brown ears.

Insert a brown pipe cleaner (you can color a white one with coffee) at the back of the tube body and glue into place. Glue four large wooden beads or four small empty spools of thread in the front and back for the legs.

Have friends sign their names on the long body. This is a good gift for children and for hospital patients.

MOLE TOY

Find a remnant of fake fur in the fabric shop. Cut in the shape of a mole. Sew up three sides and stuff with small bit of foam. Remember that a mole is on the slim side. Be sure to make his nose very pointy.

Sew tiny ears with bits of gray felt on either side of the head. Take pink felt and sew a tiny mouth at the bottom of the head. Sew small black eyes on either side of the head; also, sew a piece of pink felt for a short tail.

Chapter 6
Group Fund Raising Projects

Many of you belong to organizations. You sometimes run out of ideas and have to search for new ways of making money for your group. Here is a chapter devoted to the raising of money in a fun way by using many of the leftovers from the work basket, the workbench and home throw-aways. Folks enjoy purchasing practical gifts in a low price range, which is a help to the organization to stay alive (Fig. 6-1).

BIKE BACKPACK

Use ½ yard of canvas or duck fabric. Fold it in half. Stitch up the sides so it will be strong by using a sewing machine or sewing by hand with heavy buttonthread.

Turn over the top of the bag and hem the fabric with tiny stitches, leaving the top open. Stitch small curtain rings around the top and draw a thong or heavy nylon cord through the rings.

Hang the item on your back when you are on a bike hike. It is good for holding lunch and collecting specimens (Fig. 6-2).

CAR BAG

Take two pieces of material such as burlap or upholstery fabric. Decide on the measurements of the bag. It could be 12" × 12" or double, depending on how large you wish.

Lay the material on the table and sketch a design with a piece of chalk:—maybe a bird, rabbit, flower or your initials. Cut according to your measurements and sew together, folding in half the three sides with the chain or back stitch and using a big

Fig. 6-1. Some fund raising ideas.

embroidery needle and heavy duty thread or cord. If you wish, sew it on the sewing machine for it will hold longer. Turn over the top about 1½" wide for the drawstring. Slit an opening for the drawstring.

Take a strong piece of cord or string and draw through the opening with a safety pin. Be sure to sew closed where the string enters the top of the bag. The car bag is a nice place to keep lunch, games, puzzles, toys and treasures collected on a trip (Fig. 6-3).

Fig. 6-2. Bike backpack.

Fig. 6-3. Car bag.

MARBLE BAG

Take a piece of strong material and cut a square 6" × 6". Turn over edges ½" and sew, leaving an opening for drawstring. Carefully gather up the ends of material and slip a strong cord through the place left for the drawstring. Sew the ends of the cords together with strong button thread (Fig. 6-4).

Fig. 6-4. Marble bag.

Fig. 6-5. Fabric crayon craft.

FABRIC CRAYON CRAFT

Purchase a package of crayons. Draw a design on a piece of white paper and color in the design.

Choose a synthetic fabric if you wish the design to be permanent. Place the fabric on a towel on the ironing board or table. Lay a paper design face down onto the fabric. Set the iron to cotton setting, and use a clean sheet or paper between the iron and paper design.

Turn on the iron and use a steady pressure with iron for a few minutes. Remove the design paper gently. The colored design will be transferred onto the fabric.

You can machine wash the article if you turn the gauge on gentle action and use warm water. This crayon craft can be used on a scarf, kerchief, pillow cover, under glass as a picture or on your favorite T-shirt (Fig. 6-5).

MUFFIN TIN CADDY

Buy an inexpensive muffin tin or use an old one at home. Paint it with a bright colored enamel. Use it in the sewing room for pins, in the desk drawer for paper clips, rubber bands and stamps, and in the bureau drawer for bobby pins and jewelry.

BOTTLE LADY

Fill an empty detergent bottle with water or sand. Screw the top on tightly.

Cover the bottle with wallpaper paste or use flour and water as a paste. Cut strips of newspaper, moisten with flour paste and apply to the bottle. If you want a fat lady, add extra layers of newspaper strips. Be sure to let each layer dry completely before adding the second layer.

Build up the newspaper and paste to make a head, rounding it as you form the head over the cap of the bottle. Dry well and then begin to paint the lady's face. Use yarn for the hair and add a small hat if you wish by cutting fabric and gluing it onto the hair.

Take a piece of fabric from the work basket. Cut a skirt, dipping it into the paste and wrapping it around the lady. Do the same by fashioning a blouse. Spray the doll with a clear plastic spray (Figs. 6-6 and 6-7).

CUP AND SAUCER MAN

Take an old plastic saucer and cup. Glue the cup to the saucer.

Decorate the front of the cup in the face of a man. Use black felt for eyes and eyebrows, a piece of yellow felt for the nose and a

Fig. 6-6. Note the size and shape of the bottle used for this project.

bit of red felt for the mouth. Glue a piece of black felt for a mustache over the mouth.

Glue bits of rickrack around the rim to make it attractive. Place an arrangement of artificial flowers in clay or a real live plant in the cup (Fig. 6-8).

GOURD RATTLE

In the fall of the year, use a dry gourd. Cut off the top of the gourd carefully, and fill the gourd with dried beans, peas or small pebbles.

Glue the top of the gourd back in place. If there is a stem, use it as a handle and tie to it the other thongs, or dark colored shoe-strings. If you have no gourds, you can make a rattle out of a tin can or cardboard box and fill them with small pebbles (Fig. 6-9).

COFFEE CAN BANKS

Take an empty coffee can with a plastic lid. Cut a slot in the plastic lid of the can. Cover the coffee can with gay pieces of felt

Fig. 6-7. The dressed bottle lady.

Fig. 6-8. The completed cup and saucer man.

glued onto the can or use contact paper. Trim with rickrack, bits of lace and ribbon. Give as a gift with this saying attached, "I am your bank. Fill up my tank." See Fig. 6-10.

Fig. 6-9. Gourd rattle.

Fig. 6-10. Coffee can bank.

SWIRL JAR

Take an old kettle and fill it with water, three-fourths full. Use your leftover colored paints and pour them into the water.

Fig. 6-11. Swirl jar.

249

Fig. 6-12. Button art.

Take a pretty glass jar and gently lower it so that the outside will touch the surface of the water. Turn it slowly and be sure the whole jar has been dipped.

Remove the jar and let it dry thoroughly. You can use this ornamental jar for a pencil holder or flower holder (Fig. 6-11).

BUTTON ART

Choose a large button as big as a 50-cent piece from your botton jar. Insert a piece of clay in the center of the button as big as a pea.

Fig. 6-13. Milkweed pod picture.

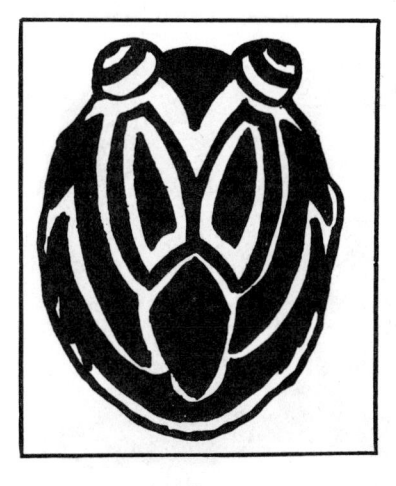

Fig. 6-14. A stone bug paperweight.

Use miniature straw flowers, dried weeds found beside the roadside or artificial flowers found in a store. Stick them into the clay in an attractive manner. These make simple gifts for shut-ins (Fig. 6-12).

MILKWEED POD PICTURE

Gather some milkweed pods in the fall. Clean out the white fuzz and lay the pods out to dry.

Find some small acorns, pine cones and burrs. A few thin sticks are needed for this project.

Find an old picture frame in the attic or at a garage sale. Remove the glass. Paint the back of the frame with a warm brown paint. You can cover the wood back with burlap by gluing.

Fig. 6-15. A red brook clay panda.

251

Fig. 6-16. A red brook clay bear.

Take four to five halves of pods and arrange them like the petals of a flower in the center of the background. Glue them fast when they please you. Glue a small pine cone in the center. Spray with gold or let the arrangement be natural.

Take one of the thin sticks and arrange it in a slight curve for the stem. Glue it fast (Fig. 6-31).

Fig. 6-17. Reminder board.

Fig. 6-18. Soda carrier tote bag.

STONE BUG PAPERWEIGHT

Find a stone, fairly smooth, about 3" × 2". Draw a design of a bug and color with bright colored enamels. Glue two movable eyes in front. Use black pipe cleaners for legs. Flatten the ends so that they will glue under the bottom of the bug (Fig. 6-14).

BROOK CLAY FIGURES

Scoop out clay from the creek bed and lay it on a tray. Pick out all the dirt and strain it through an old sieve if necessary.

Mold the figures by hand, rolling the clay into pencil-like strips. Coil them around in a circle for the base and then on up to the top for making a vase. Or you can use big chunks of clay for forming the articles you wish. Be sure to use a lot of water to keep clay workable. Let the creations dry in the sunshine in a warm location.

Remember that the red brook clay is very fragile and brittle when dry, whereas the yellowish and white clay is heavier and makes stronger articles. Store extra clay in a plastic bag well moistened. Never let it dry out (Figs. 6-15 and 6-16).

Fig. 6-19. A tree-shaped candle.

Fig. 6-20. A ball-shaped candle.

REMINDER BOARD

Secure a piece of cork or lightweight plywood from a lumber mill. Paint the plywood your favorite color. Glue bright colored pieces of yarn, rickrack or leather strips around the rectangle.

Make two holes at the top of the board. Hang a heavy cord through the holes to hang on the wall. If your board is made of cork, make one hole and hang a cord through the hole.

On the cork board you can glue any designs you wish to make it attractive. Use cutouts from magazines or seals from the stationery store.

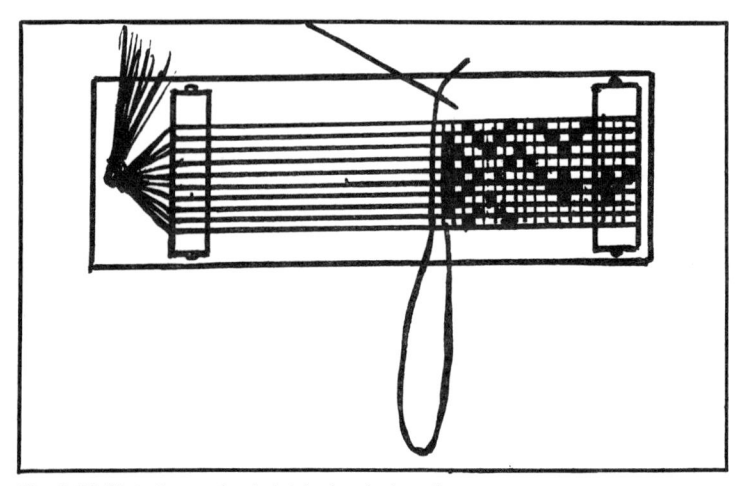

Fig. 6-21. Note the method of stringing the beads.

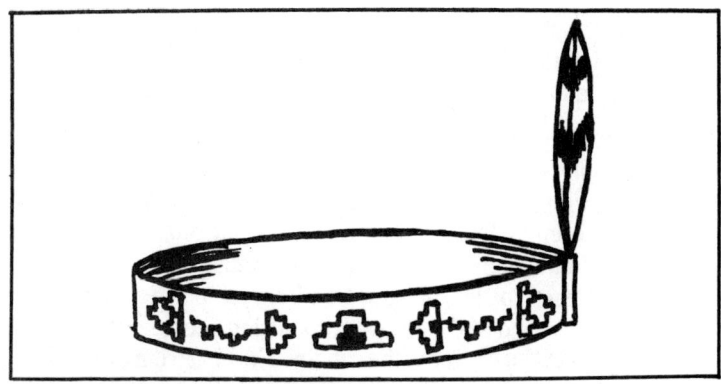

Fig. 6-22. The completed Indian headband.

Purchase a box of thumbtacks for hanging notes. It is handy to hang a pencil beside the board. The pencil can be attached to a string held by a tack or hook (Fig. 6-17).

SODA CARRIER TOTE BOX

Use one of your old soda carriers and paint with acrylic paint on the inside and outside. After paint has dried, draw an attractive design on the front and on the back of the carrier.

Put a paper or plastic cup into each bottle slot. Here you can store crayons, scissors, pencils, rulers and glue bottles. They make great picnic totes for knives, forks and spoons, etc. For bedfast patients, the box holds their necessities (Fig. 6-18).

EASY CANDLEMAKING

You will need paraffin and some of your old candles, colored wax crayons, assorted shaped plastic dishes, cookie cutters, small

Fig. 6-23. A wooden bead bird.

jello molds, an egg beater, knives, an old saucepan (I like the double boiler for safety first), spool wire, and some long steel knitting needles or long skewers.

Cut up your candles. Save all the old wicks. Fill about one-half of the double boiler full of old candles. Melt them, stirring frequently with an old knife. Choose the colors you wish by scraping different colors of crayons into the hot wax, stirring until melted. Set out your molds. Pour the wax into molds and let harden. It is easy to slip the hard wax from the plastic mold. Now heat the pointed end of the skewer or knitting needle over a flame and insert it into the center of the candle. The heat from the skewer will melt the wax and enable you to fasten a wick to a piece of the spool wire. Pull the spool wire through the hole in the candle and the wick will slide through. Trim off the excess wick. Seal at the top and at the bottom of the candle by dropping some hot wax over the openings.

To make an evergreen tree or a snowball, remove the hot wax from the stove and wait until it sets. This takes a few minutes. Then take the egg beater and whip until it is frothy, white and slightly rough, but not completely hard. Scoop up the wax and place it where you desire. Do not make the wax smooth or it will lose its snowy appearance. To get a marble-like candle, pack candle molds with two or three different shades of whipped wax. If you want a round candle, you can cut a rubber ball in half and pour the hot wax into each half. When the wax is hard, remove semicircular candles from molds and use hot wax to seal dripping around the center.

The old fashioned way of dripping candles is fun and easy to do. Attach wicks to a strong support like a lightweight piece of pipe or dowel. Tie the sicks to the support, and let them hang down as long as you want your candle to be. Attach a heavy nut to the end of the wick to hold them in place.

Cook up your wax using a large container because you will dip about four wicks into the kettle. Then let them dry a few minutes. Repeat the dipping process until you have the candle of the desired thickness. Cut off the nut or weight and you have a candle to be proud of.

If you have an old fashioned candle mold, use it by filling the molds with hot wax. Slip the wicks down into the center with a weight and hang the wicks onto a stick tied up to a support (Figs. 6-19 and 6-20).

INDIAN HEADBAND

Purchase a wooden loom which takes up to 77 bead width. The dowels permit up to 40" long beadwork; you can get longer dowels for longer work. You can buy the metal loom which is a strong heavy gauge loom and takes up to 36 beads wide. The length rolls up on the spool.

For an Indian headband, design on graph paper your Indian design using books from the library to find the correct symbols. Each square on the paper is a bead, and it is easy to count the lines and pattern a design.

Usually a border is woven on either side to bring out the background and design. Use good bright colors.

Seed beads may be purchased in various colors by the pound or by the vial. Buy beading needles and strong nylon thread. String your loom counting the strings according to the width you plan to make your headband.

Place your different colored seed beads in small margarine containers. Slip your threaded single strand needle into the seed beads counting your design. Then take up the beads on the thread and hold them under the strings on the loom so that each bead will stand up through each string. Take your needle and gently slip it through the beads and over the thread. When you come to the end of the row, take a bobby pin and check if you caught every bead by pulling up on the thread. If the bead is not locked into place, slip out the needle and try again.

Pull the thread through and go on to the next line. Continue on until your design is completed. Then take one color bead and separate the designs with this row. Weave six symbols and turn the loom as needed for new threads.

When completed, take it off of the loom, measure your head size, and cut a piece of soft suede leather for backing. Allow an extra few inches of suede for fastening. Turn in strings and trim long ones. Sew suede to the edges of the headband. Punch two holes in one end of the suede backing. Cut a few strips of suede about 2" long and knot one in each hole. Then punch two more holes on the other end of the suede backing and fasten pieces of suede and knot. When you try the band around your head, you can tie the two strings together. Make the suede backing longer so you can tie it at the back of your head. Punch two holes at the ends. Use a leather thong or soft piece of cut leather to tie to the other punched holed end of the headband (Figs. 6-21 and 6-22).

Fig. 6-24. A wooden bead mushroom.

WOODEN BEAD FOLKS AND WILDLIFE

Buy some assorted wooden beads in a craft shop. Hunt up a smooth small rock, preferably one from the creek bed that has rounded edges. Make a bird by using a large round bead and gluing a smaller bead on top for the head.

Cut tiny pieces of pipe cleaners using yellow for the feet. Glue the feet to the large bead. Glue a feather in the back of the body for the tail. Attach two small pieces of yellow construction paper for the beak on the face. Perch the bird on the stone and glue securely.

Make a mushroom or two out of a large wooden bead cut in half for the cap. Use an oblong bead for the stem. Glue small bits of artificial foilage around bead creations.

Get out your paints and brushes. Paint the bird a face and the mushrooms a cap. You can use your imagination and create many wooden bead scenes (Figs. 6-23 and 6-24).

CLAY FLOWERS

Purchase some flower clay at a hobby shop. Try a rose.

Roll out a ball of clay. For different sizes of roses, you may use larger or smaller balls of clay. Flatten the ball into a flat circle of clay, and leave it thicker at the bottom.

Make the petals very wafer-like, thin and dainty at their edges. Pinch the edges of the flower with your finger and thumb. When the edges are wafer-thin, roll the circle into a roll.

Keep adding petals until you have the flower you desire. Then trim off excess clay. Let it dry for a day.

Try a daisy. Roll a small ball and flatten leaving a slight hump for the center. Roll out the clay, cut petals and press to the center.

Make the flower as large as you wish. Attach a green floristic wire stem and let the clay dry. You can paint the flower in color or let it be natural.

TOTEM POLE

Choose a good solid oak tree, large in size. Saw it down and lay it on two sawhorses, fastening them with large spikes so the tree will not roll. Strip off all the bark using a two-handled drawknife.

On a paper, draw up a design that you would like. Indian symbols tell a story. You can get ideas in a Camp Fire Girls' manual or borrow a book from the library on Indian symbols.

Fig. 6-25. Totem pole.

Fig. 6-26. A bird paperweight made of shells and a stone.

Sketch on your designs with pencil and then magic markers. Take a chisel and small hammer. Carve out the symbols cutting about ½" deep into the wood. Your design will be raised. You may want to sand rough edges. Paint the background an outside white or cream colored paint.

Paint the symbols bright Indian colors: yellow, green, blue, orange, black, scarlet and brown. Use an outside enamel and a good grade paint. Outlining designs in black makes them outstanding. As you work around the totem pole, you will have to roll the log on the sawhorses so that the designs are all around the pole.

When all art work is completed, you are ready to plant the pole. Dig a hole 1½ to 2 feet deep depending on the size of the pole. Paint the end of the pole that fits into the hole with creosote to protect wood. Cover up and tamp down well.

If you are really ambitious, it is fun to round off the top of the pole into a head for the thunderbird. Make it the size of a small round pumpkin. Take two pieces of wood about 8" long and carve out two wings. Be sure to make the outside of the wing jagged, by using a knife and carving a *scallop* 2" apart. Fasten the inner part of the wing to the bottom of the neck where the head starts to form; use bolts or long screws. Decorate the head with two glass knobs, found in a hardware shop, that will screw into the wood. Carve a nose and paint on the mouth. This makes a good Camp Fire, Boy or Girl Scout project, or a nice ornament for a country cabin.

To make mini-totem poles, use soft pine wood from scraps from a lumber mill. Carve with a pocket knife, using the same method as used for a large totem pole. Use them for favors or gifts (Fig. 6-25).

ROCK FUN

Find a smooth rock along the roadside, in the woods or in a creek bed. Scrub it well and dry thoroughly.

For decoration, you can paint a design such as a rabbit, bird or girl in a sunbonnet on the top of the rock. Or glue a rock body to the flat rock base, using a strong glue. Put a heavy weight on the stones so that they will hold together.

Use two buttons or seed beads and glue them in place for the eyes. Use a small red button or piece of jewelry for the mouth.

For a bird paperweight, you can glue two shells to the sides of the stone for the wings. Using imagination makes working with rock fun (Fig. 6-26).

SHELL BIRD

Glue two angel wing shells together for the body with a pipe cleaner between one end for the neck. Insert the pipe cleaner in the open side of the shell for the head. Glue two pipe cleaners on the outside of the shell for legs. Cut paper webbed feet of orange paper. Bend the pipe cleaners at the bottom and paste the feet over them.

Glue the bird to a wooden base. You can add very small movable eyes to the head, a few feathers for a tail and a small feather to the top of the head.

SEED FUN

Save all seeds from fruits and dry them in the sunshine or a slow oven. Use seeds from watermelons, cantaloupes, sunflowers, beans, peas, etc.

After the seeds are well dried, string them on heavy nylon thread, using an embroidery needle. If you wish to paint them, do this before stringing. You can create bracelets, necklaces and seed pictures. Storing the dried seeds in jars allows you to work on this project when you wish.

SEED PICTURE

Choose a piece of scrap wood ¼" thick from the workbench, measuring 8 × 8 or any size you wish. Varnish it a dark brown.

Sand edges smooth and apply glue around the edges of the wooden base. Press an ornamental cord, rickrack or twine down on the glued place. This will frame the picture. Take a pencil and sketch a design in the center of the wood.

Apply glue and add vegetables, flower seeds, macaroni, rice, dried beans and sunflower seeds. A variety of seeds makes the picture interesting. For a horse's head, use pea and radish seeds for his mane, and a lima bean for his eye. Fasten a metal screw eye on the back of the picture for hanging.

PAPER PLATE DECOR

Take an ordinary paper plate and draw in the center a design of a flower or fern. Cut construction paper in colors you wish to match the design you have drawn. Glue the colored designs onto the paper plate.

You can paint the plate a solid base color or leave it white. You can trim around the plate using paint or colored seals.

Chapter 7
Items for
Wildlife and Pets

We all enjoy the wildlife in our woodlands and fields. In this chapter you will find easy ways to urge the birds to remain on your property all year long. For the pets in your homes, there are simple crafts that can be made to make them happy and comfortable (Fig. 7-1).

TIN CAN BIRD FEEDER

Lay the can lengthwise in front of you. Take an empty 16-ounce can. Cut and remove either end of the can. Paint the can white.

Cut the plastic lids in half. Bore a hole in the upper part of each half and push the lids on either end of the can. Push an 8″ × 12″ perching stick through the hole in one end of the plastic lids through the inside of the can to the other end.

Fill the can with grain and hang it up in a tree lengthwise by a piece of wire punched into the top of the can. Decorate the top with a piece of artificial holly (Fig. 7-2).

CHICKADEE FEEDER

Take a small log and drill holes into the log almost halfway through. Mix up a bird cake and press it into the hole. Peanut butter and crumbs may be spooned into holes. Add a hook on top of the log and hang in a tree (Fig. 7-3).

BOTTLE BIRD FEEDER

Take a ½ gallon *Clorox* bottle and cut a hole in the front 3″ to 4″ high from the bottom of the bottle and 3″ to 4″ wide. Hang it up in

Fig. 7-1. These are some items that pets will be sure to love.

the tree by the head of the bottle with strong twine, or attach to the trunk of a tree by the handle with strong cord. Put bird feed into the opening (Fig. 7-4).

GOURD BIRDHOUSE

Harvest a *Hercules Club* or any large gourd from the garden. Before it is dried out, carve a small hole about 3" up from the bottom as large as a quarter to house a wren.

Dry the gourd well and spar varnish or shellac it for preservation. Next spring, hang it up in a tree by a cord tied tightly around the gourd's neck.

To make a water dipper, cut in half the body of the gourd, leaving the stem on for the handle. Do not varnish. This is only for the Hercules Club type (Fig. 7-5).

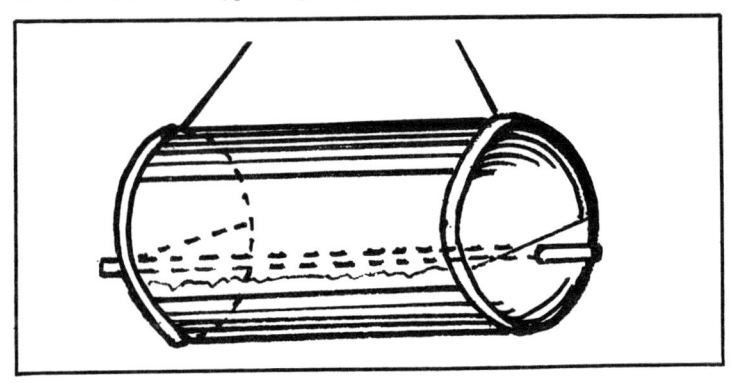

Fig. 7-2. Tin can bird feeder.

WOODEN WREN HOUSE

Use hardboard with the rough side on the outside. Cut three pieces of hardboard ¼" thick, 5" × 5". Cut two more 7" × 5". On the longer pieces, draw lines from the center of the long side to each side 5" up from the bottom. Cut off the triangles. This will give you the peak to the house. Glue and nail to opposite sides of the one 5" square that will be the floor. Glue and nail the other two sides to the house.

In the front side of the house, drill a hole 3" up from the bottom no larger than a quarter, or sparrows will try to use it. About ½" below the hole, drill a ¼" hole and glue into that a ¼" dowel stick 1½" long for a perch.

For the roof, you can get bark slabs that are used in large plants to help hold them up. Cut into two pieces 4" × 6". Miter one side of the 6" lengths. They will dovetail together at the peak of the roof. Glue and nail together. Glue and nail the roof to the sides of the house. Put a large hook in the middle to hang it by (Fig. 7-6).

SUET BASKETS AND BIRD CAKES

Use empty orange or onion sacks and fill with hunks of *suet* or fat found at a butcher shop. Close the end with a cord and hang it up in a tree. This keeps the birds warm in the winter time.

For bird cakes, melt down fat in a pan and add peanut butter, bits of bread, leftover vegetables and bird seed. Pour the mixture

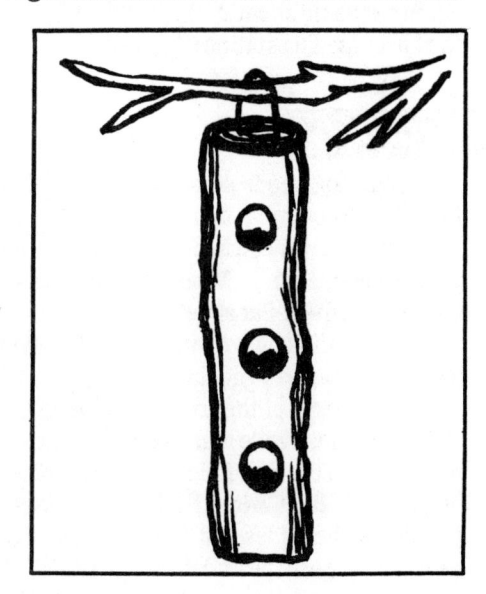

Fig. 7-3. Chickadee feeder.

Fig. 7-4. Plastic bottle feeder.

out in a cake tin about 2" thick and cool. Cut into squares and lay on the birds' feeding station (Fig. 7-7).

DOG COLLAR

Your dog needs some protection when he goes out at night. Make him a dog collar that will be good looking and useful, too.

Either buy a cheap plain dog collar or get some scrap leather from a shoe factory. Measure your dog's neck and allow for the buckle. Cut the collar about 2" wide.

Attach the buckle with a rivet or two if needed. Punch holes for the buckle part to go through.

Buy a strip of the iridescent foil used on automobiles. Cut a strip a little less wide than the collar, but long enough to reach from the buckle to the first hole. Also, buy some reflective tape used on bicycles, about 1" wide. Both tapes comes with adhesive backing, so adhere the iridescent foil first. Put the narrower strip of red reflective tape in the middle of that (Fig. 7-8).

Fig. 7-5. Gourd bird house.

CAT COLLAR

Cats need the protection more so than dogs because they are allowed to run freely. Make the collar the same as the dog collar as far as the leather is concerned, but don't make it more than 1" wide.

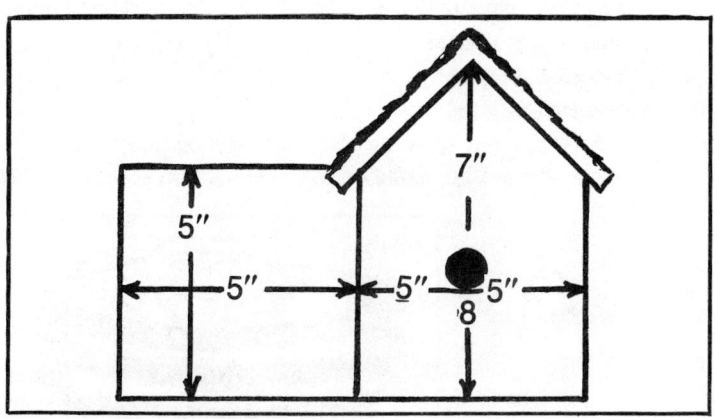

Fig. 7-6. Wooden wren house.

Fig. 7-7. A tree treat for birds.

The red strip should be much narrower. You can cut out the semblance of a small bow for the front and attach it.

Punch two small holes in the center of the bow. These holes will hold two small bells that hang from the collar. This is a very good thing to do, especially if you love birds. The birds will hear the bells and not be surprised by a hungry cat (Fig. 7-9).

DECORATED DOG DISH

Whether your dog's dinner dish is metal or plastic doesn't matter, but if you put his name on it you show him that you love

Fig. 7-8. Dog collar.

268

Fig. 7-9. Cat collar.

him. Cut letters of different sizes and colors from old magazines. Glue them on the dog dish in a haphazard design. Use glue especially made for either metal or plastic. When the glue has thoroughly dried, give the outside of the dish a coat of clear acrylic paint. In fact, you might give it two coats because you know his dish will be washed a lot (Fig. 7-10).

DOG BLANKET

You can make this blanket out of scraps of wool material that you have around the house, or buy a small piece of wool or felt. Make a pattern by using brown wrapping paper wrapped around the dog to get the size. As you can see by Fig. 7-11, it is fastened on the dog by overlapping the front with a button or snap. It does not go under the dog's tummy but connects with a strap. The strap can be of the same material as the dog's coat. Sew a buckle on one end. Punch holes in the other end so you can snap or buckle it on. If you want to be very fancy, you can sew or glue the dog's name on the top of another color of felt.

CATNIP BAG

Choose a material that is not too thick and will allow your cat to smell the catnip through it. Make it like a small bean bag, about

Fig. 7-10. Personalized dog dish.

Fig. 7-11. Dog blanket.

3" square. Sew up three sides, insert the catnip, fold the last edge under and sew closed. Your cat will have many hours of pleasure from it (Fig. 7-12).

BIRD CAGE COVER

Measure around the cage. If the cage is round, cut a circle big enough to wrap around the cage and overlap, and long enough to come down the sides but not cut off air. Cut a small circle out of the top. Bind around the edges with bias binding and use *Velcro* for the closing.

Fig. 7-12. Catnip bag.

Fig. 7-13. Bird cage cover.

If the cage is oblong, cut two pieces longer than the sides and two pieces longer than the ends. Cut an oblong piece for the top. Sew together like a cover for a toaster with binding on the seams. Use Velcro for closing (Fig. 7-13).

SCRATCH POST FOR A CAT

Find a limb of a tree that is about 3" in diameter and about 12" long. Cover with medium sandpaper. Get a large thick piece of tree trunk from the lumber company. Put a long nail up through the center and through the limb. Your cat can keep his nails trimmed (Fig. 7-14).

Fig. 7-14. Scratching post for a cat.

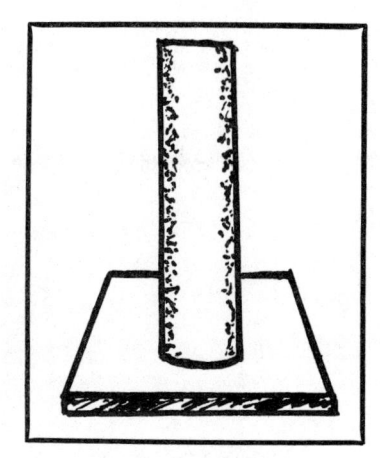

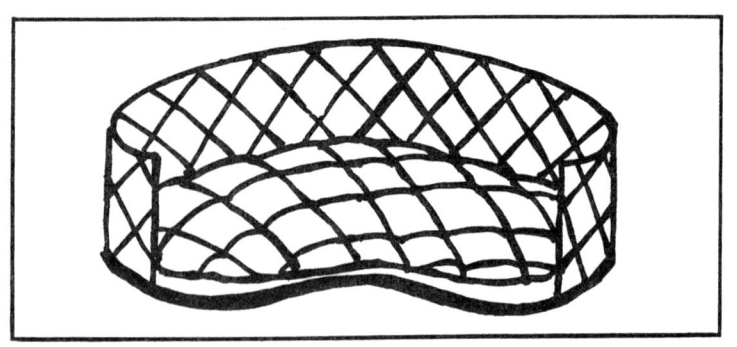

Fig. 7-15. A dog or cat bed.

DOG OR CAT BED

Cut from 1" thick lumber a curved shape as shown (Fig. 7-15). Make sure it is big enough for your pet so that he will not be cramped—add about 2" to the back and sides for uprights.

Drill ½" holes about 3" apart around the back and sides of the base. Insert ½" dowels about 5 or 6" long.

Measure and cut from quilted material a piece long enough and wide enough to go over the dowels front and back. Sew together at the ends and bind with bias binding. Slip over the dowels.

Measure and cut two pieces of quilted material big enough to cover the base. Sew them together and bind edges with bias binding. Cover the base. By making them in separate pieces it is easier to remove them for washing.

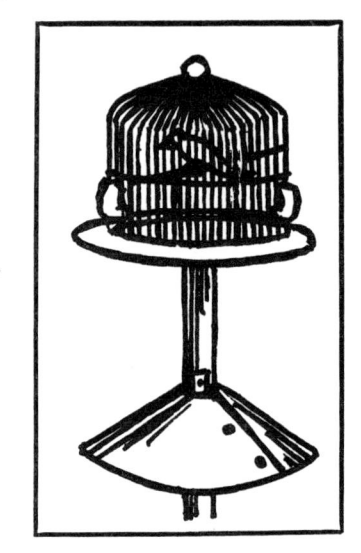

Fig. 7-16. Mouse repellent for a bird cage.

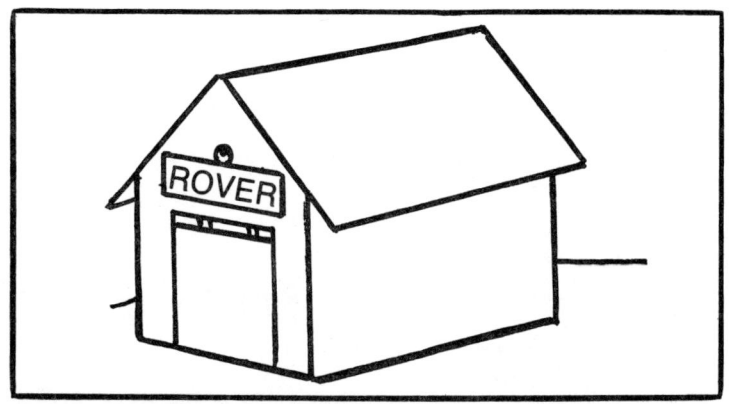

Fig. 7-17. A comfortable house for your dog.

MOUSE REPELLENT FOR A BIRD CAGE

Mice love bird seed. Unfortunately, their droppings resemble some seeds. If birds eat them, they will die. Make a collar for your cage, especially if it is on a pole since mice can climb.

Cut a piece of tin into a three fourths of a circle shape. Make it at least 12" in diameter. Cut a circle from the center big enough to wrap around the pole and overlap enough to fasten. Leave two tabs on for fastening to the pole as shown, and bend up (Fig. 7-16).

Drill two holes in the pole and the same size holes in the tabs. Wrap the tin around the pole first so you know where to drill holes on the pole. Drill holes in the ends of the circle of tin so that they can be fastened together with a nut and screw or riveted.

Place tin around the pole. Attach to the pole and fasten the ends together.

DOG HOUSE

Measure your dog and make sure his house will be big enough so that he can turn around in it and lie down in comfort. Cut the base and sides from hardboard about ¾" thick. Cut out the door. Make sure it is big enough. The door can be hung from two rings so that it will swing open or shut. Nail and glue the sides, front and back together first. The floor should be of a heavier wood about 1" thick. Glue and nail the sides and front to the base from the bottom up. Put a piece of rug inside for a little warmth (Fig. 7-17).

Chapter 8
Just For Fun Crafts

There are so many ways in which to have a good time in the "do-it-yourself world." Family fun can be found by creating crafts.

In this day of inflation, more interesting and inexpensive entertainment must be discovered. Creations of easy crafts will strengthen family ties and leave good memories of home life (Fig. 8-1).

SPOOL TOYS

Save empty spools of thread. For the baby, string them on a white shoe string.

For the tinker toy, glue large empty spools on top of each other to form a man. Glue two small spools on either side for the arms.

Paint the spool man in bright red enamel. Use black enamel on the top spool to decorate the face (Fig. 8-2).

ICE HOCKEY PUCK

Take an empty tuna fish can. Fill it with a plaster of paris mixture. Carefully level off the top. Paint the can black or bright red (Fig. 8-3).

BROOMSTICK HORSE

Find an old broomstick. Saw off the old broom. Sand down and paint a bright color.

Cut a small horse's head from a piece of foam rubber. Be sure to include a piece for the neck to fit over the broomstick. Cover the head and neck with bright colored fabric.

Fig. 8-1. Some just for fun ideas.

Sew two black buttons on either side of the head for the eyes, two pieces of black felt for the ears, two small pieces of black felt for the nostrils and one red piece for the mouth. Stick the head over the broomstick and fasten to the neck with a tight cord by stapling (Fig. 8-4).

BEAN BOARD BACKDROP

Use a board about 24" × 36" at least, about ½" thick. Put a hinge at the top in the middle that will hold a stick ½"-3"-36". Put a point on the end. Paint a clown's face on the front board, cutting out a mouth that will be big enough for a bean bag to go through easily.

Fig. 8-2. Spool toy.

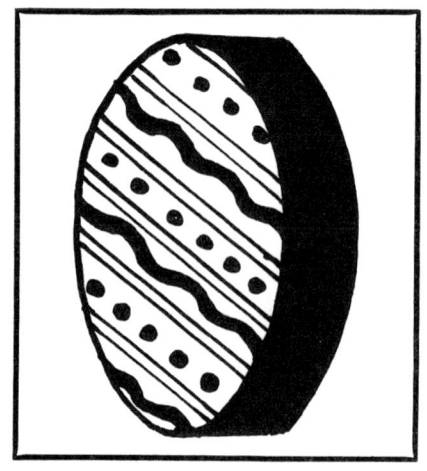

Fig. 8-3. Ice hockey puck.

Paint the face white, the eyes blue and the nose and around the mouth red. Place the pointed end in the ground so the board is on a slant (Fig. 8-5).

STILTS

Find 2½" × 2" wood strips about 5 feet long. Secure two blocks of 2" × 3" lumber.

Fig. 8-4. The completed broomstick horse.

Hunt up two old leather men's belts. They should be 1½" wide × 5" long. Nail one on each stilt from the strip down to the side of the block. Be sure to leave enough room for your foot to fit loosely.

Sand the stilts and varnish or paint them. Then the trick is to learn to balance and walk upon them smoothly (Fig. 8-6).

SAND SHOVEL

Find a ½ gallon empty bleach bottle. Poke the point of your scissors into the bottle about 1" up from the bottom. Cut the bottom of the bleach bottle.

Lay down the bleach bottle so the handle is facing upward. Find the center of the handle and measure down 5" on both sides. Mark the center back of the bottle in the same manner.

Using your scissors, cut a rectangle by cutting A to B, B to D, D to C and C to A. You can trim and curve your corners of the so-called scoop with your scissors.

The shovel is an inexpensive way to have fun at the beach or in the sandbox for the child making a sand castle. It is also handy for the gardener (Fig. 8-7).

Fig. 8-5. Bean board backdrop.

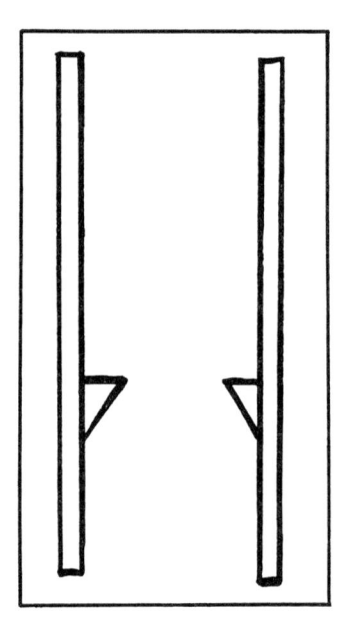

Fig. 8-6. These stilts are fun to use.

HORSE TAIL

Use a large empty spool of thread. Take four small finishing nails or braids about ½" long. Hammer the nails at equal distances around the top.

Take an end of yarn from a ball or skein and tie it around the first nail. Hold the spool in your hand and wind the yarn, alternating around the rest of the nails two times, making a square.

Slip up the first strand of yarn over the second strand onto the nails. This starts the weaving of the horse tail. As the yarn is pulled up through the hole and you see it is getting to the end, just tie another piece of yarn at the end.

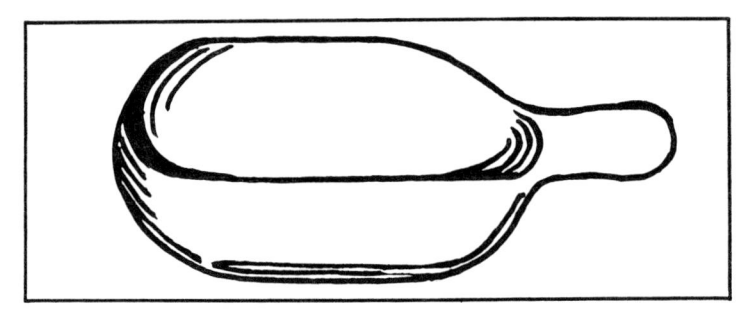

Fig. 8-7. Use a bleach bottle to make the sand shovel.

After you have woven the horse tail, take it off the spool and coil it in a circle. Sew it together with strong thread and a needle. Use it as a hot dish holder, place mat, pot holder, or as a small rug for a dollhouse, or a mat under a lamp (Fig. 8-8).

RHYTHM STICKS

Use dowels about 12″ long and ½″ thick. Sand them down; decorate them as you wish. Then clear varnish or shellac them. Use them like drumsticks and click them together. Plain sticks do not have the ring that shellacked sticks have. Children love rhythm sticks to keep time to music.

TREE HOUSE

Find three to four large limbs on a tree. Attach 2 × 4s for supports to these big branches. Nail heavy floor boards to the supports. Of course, the size of the tree house depends on the size of the tree and branch span.

Fig. 8-8. Horse tail braid.

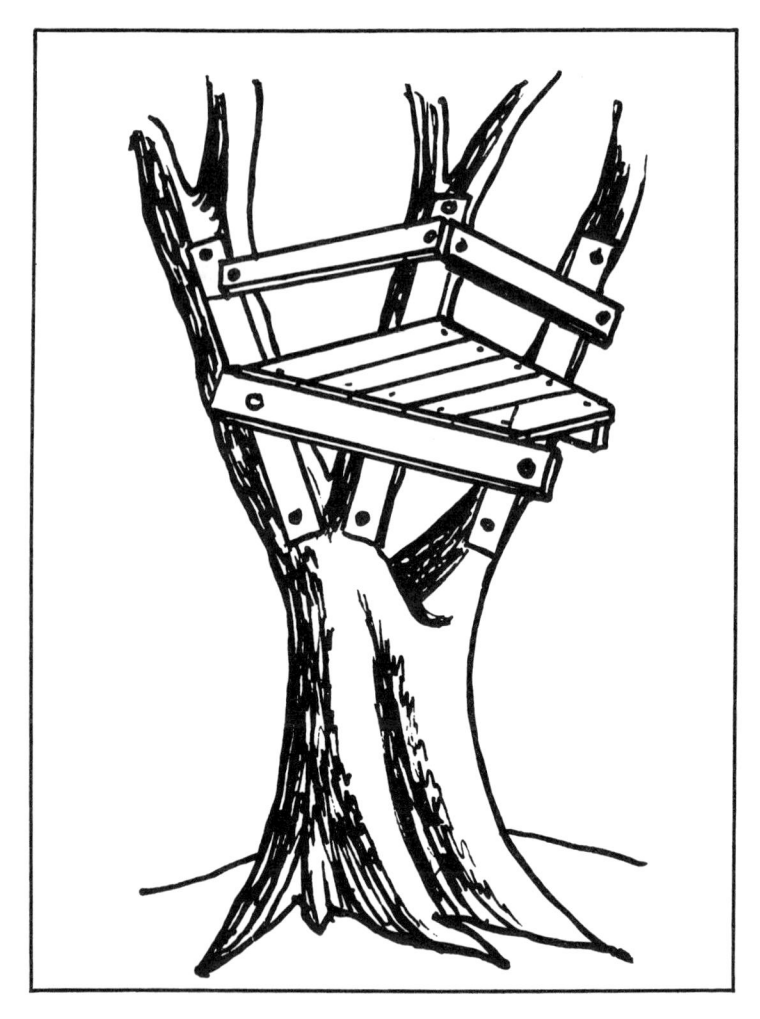

Fig. 8-9. Youngsters will have a good time playing in this tree house.

Attach 3-foot-high 2 × 4s to each corner of the floor of the tree house. To these side supports, nail 2 × 4s or 2 × 3s so there is a good sturdy railing.

Leave the side open and build a stairway down to the ground. A good strong ladder nailed to the supports of the floor works well (Fig. 8-9).

PINE CONE TOYS

Gather some pine cones from evergreen trees. Take a pine cone and add pieces of cardboard stuck into the cone for a head and

Fig. 8-10. Use twigs or pipe cleaners for the bird's legs.

ears. Use a small cone on a large cone for the body and head. Use a piece of bird feather or chicken feather for the tail.

Pieces of twigs or pipe cleaners work well for legs. Glue the beaks, heads, tails and legs for a longer-lasting effect (Fig. 8-10).

PLAY BLOCKS

Visit a lumber mill and purchase some pieces of wood. Take them home and cut them about 4″ long, 3″ wide and 2″ thick. If you have leftover pieces of wood at home, use them.

Sand the blocks well and paint them with a good solid color. If you are an artist, paint pictures of animals on the top of the blocks or cut out pictures from magazines. Paste them on top of the block.

Fig. 8-11. A panda decorates this play block.

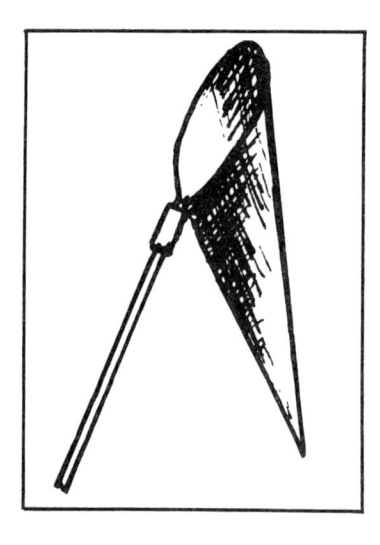

Fig. 8-12. Butterfly net.

Spar varnish the whole block. These blocks make great gifts for toddlers. They learn their animals from playing with the blocks (Fig. 8-11).

BUTTERFLY NET

Take a lightweight wire coat hanger and fashion it into a circle. Get a piece of mosquito netting about ½ yard and sew it into the shape of a big cone. Leave the top open and make a 2" hem to slip the piece of wire through. Sew closed the open place where the wire was inserted.

Bend two pieces of wire together with pliers. Attach a 3" dowel to the wire and bind it tight with heavy fabric tape.

July, August and September are the months to catch butterflies and moths. Catch only what you need for your collection (Fig. 8-12).

BUTTERFLY CASE

Take an empty box which is big enough for your butterfly collection. Find a piece of glass measuring about 9 × 12.

Fig. 8-13. Butterfly display box.

Fill the box with cotton one-half full, with crystals underneath or moth flakes to keep out growing larvae. The top layer of cotton is put on top, bringing batting close to the top of the box. Cut out the top of the box, leaving 2" for margin.

Lay the specimens on top of the cotton and label them with correct names. It is attractive if you add a dried weed or two to the collection.

Place the glass pane on top of the specimens, and place the top of the cut box on top of the glass. Tape either side neatly to secure the collection (Fig. 8-13).

BUTTERFLY STRETCHER

Take a soft piece of wood 10" long and 7" wide. Make a ¼" groove right through the middle lengthwise. Here is where the butterfly or moth will lie with its body in the groove.

Spred out the wings and place small strips of paper over them, secured with thumbtacks. The butterfly or moth must be put on the stretcher board as soon as it has been put to sleep. Be sure the butterfly has been in the jar for a number of hours. The butterfly will dry in this condition. Then it may be placed in its case and labeled.

Chapter 9
Recipes and
Special Techniques

In this chapter you will find recipes for clay work, drying flowers, finger paint, etc. These recipes help beat the high cost of living as simple household ingredients are mixed to use with the crafts. Also included are tips on techniques and special methods to create a simple craft.

CLAY RECIPE

Use equal amounts of cornstarch and baking soda. Place the amounts in a kettle and mix with a spoon. Slowly add water and mix until the clay is smooth.

Cook it over a slow heat for about five minutes. Remove from the stove and cool. Use your fingers to knead dough. You can roll it out with a rolling pin and cut into shapes as you wish. Let the finished shapes dry a few hours before decorating.

Paint with tempera, poster or acrylic paint. After the paint has dried, you may spray with a plastic spray or paint with clear shellac for preservation. Be sure to label the jars if you store extra clay.

RECIPE FOR SALT DOUGH CHRISTMAS TREE DECORATIONS

Mix ½ cup of cornstarch with 1 cup of salt. Add slowly ½ cup of boiling water. Mix well and knead like bread dough. Store it in a plastic bag or foil and keep it in a covered container.

You can add powdered tempera paint to the dry cornstarch and salt for color. Vegetable coloring, colored ink or tempera liquid paint added to the water work well.

Roll out the dough and cut with cookie cutters. Punch a hole with a stick or ice pick in the top for hanging on the tree. Let ornaments dry thoroughly on a tray before hanging.

RECIPE FOR SOFT CLAY FOR MODELING

You will need 2 cups of salt and 2 cups of flour (all purpose). Mix thoroughly in an old kettle with a spoon. Add water gradually to make a stiff dough. You can put out saucers of different colored food coloring, using the color you like or making a rainbow-shaded clay.

When air hits the clay it will harden, so store extra clay in jars, adding a few drops of water to keep it moist. Be sure to label the jars.

CARVING CLAY

Carving clay is as easy as carving a piece of soap. You can use this craft to make lasting novelties, figures, tiles and plaques for gift giving and for your home.

Buy clay in a hobby shop. Take a piece of paper and sketch your design with a piece of colored chalk.

Follow the directions on the package of clay. Mix the clay with water and pour it into a round oatmeal box, if you wish to have the article round. Use a long candy box for an oblong shape. Always use a larger box than the object that you will carve.

After the clay is hard, tear away the paper casting of boxes and start carving your design with a paring knife. Remember the clay will dry out quickly. Use a damp cloth to cover the object until you are finished carving.

Stroking the clay with a table knife makes the clay look like a wood carving. Then paint it with orange shellac. If you wish a smoother exterior, use sandpaper and paint with enamel, bronze or leave it a natural color.

FINGER PAINT RECIPE

Take ½ cup of laundry starch. Add 1 quart boiling water. Cool and add ¼ cup talcum powder (this helps preserve paint). Add powder or liquid poster paint for color. Stir ingredients well and pour into the glass or tight plastic jars.

RECIPE FOR DRIED FLOWER MIX

Summer and fall are the times to choose your best specimens of flower heads for drying. Here is a good inexpensive mixture to use.

Take 3 parts white cornmeal and 1 part borax. Put the mixture of cornmeal and borax in a shoe box or candy tin.

Pull off the leaves on the stem of the flower. Stick the flower head face down into the powder. Be sure to have heads completely covered.

Seal the box with tape. Let it sit for two weeks until thoroughly dried. Then shake out the flowers. Reuse the powder for other flowers. Use in arrangements in centerpieces or pictures.

BUBBLE BLOWING RECIPE

Use a quart jar mix up the following ingredients. Label the bottle. Take 2 tablespoons of soap detergent, 1 cup hot water and 1 tablespoon of glycerine.

Cool and pour a small amount into a plastic bottle to fill the pipe. Store the rest for future use.

WRAPPING PRESENTS

Save those comic strips. They make great wrapping paper for gifts. You can use the ordinary newspaper also for wrapping presents.

Visit a wallpaper shop and ask for old outdated wallpaper books. Gift tags and Christmas cards may also be made from these samples. Shelf paper or brown paper bags cut into shape and decorated with colored tape or little pictures cut out from magazines make interesting gift wrappings.

Use an empty box lid. Cover it with paper, taping the paper to the lid. Cover the box with a pretty cover.

If a member of the family likes cars, cut out car pictures and decorate plain white shelf paper. How about the old road maps? They make great wrappings for the traveler.

Wrap a present in a present. Take a cookbook and wrap it in a tea towel, wrap a doll in a doll blanket. Try giving an uncle a cookie box wrapped up in a scarf.

SCORING PAPER OR CARDBOARD

The purpose of scoring paper or cardboard is to make it easier to fold. To do this, you use a knife on cardboard, but cut only halfway through the board. On paper it is best to use a dull pointed tool or scissors keeping them closed while you make the line so that the paper is not cut. The scoring must be done on the side of the paper or board that is to fold back. If it doesn't fold easily, especially on the cardboard, score just a little deeper.

HOW TO DIVIDE CIRCLES INTO SIX AND 12 EQUAL PARTS

Decide what size you want for your outside circle. Set your compass for this and make your circle. Do not change the compass setting.

At the very top of your circle, make a dot on the circle and mark it 1. Put your compass point on this dot and swing it down until it crosses your circle with a short curve. Where that curve or arc crosses the circle, put another small dot and mark it 2.

Put your compass on that point. Swing the compass down again until it crosses the circle. Put a dot there and mark it 3.

Put your compass on dot three. Swing the compass until it crosses the circle again. Mark that dot 4. Continue around the circle until you come back to the top, making marks 5 and 6. Draw lines from those dots to the center of the circle, and you will have a circle divided into six equal parts (Fig. 9-1).

If you wish to divide each of these sections again, it is a good idea to erase the lines made by the first division. Do this so that you do not get them mixed with the lines you will make for this division.

Now you will change the compass setting, making it somewhat smaller than the first setting. Put your compass point on dot 1. Swing the compass pencil down to make a small arc, this time a little outside of the circle but close to it. Move the compass point to mark 2, and make an arc with the pencil point upward so that it crosses the other arc. Put a dot where the two arcs cross. Mark it 7. If it should not reach enough to cross the other arc, it is because you need to set the compass a little farther apart.

Move the compass point to number 2; make two arcs that cross this time between 2 and 3. Mark that dot 8. Continue on

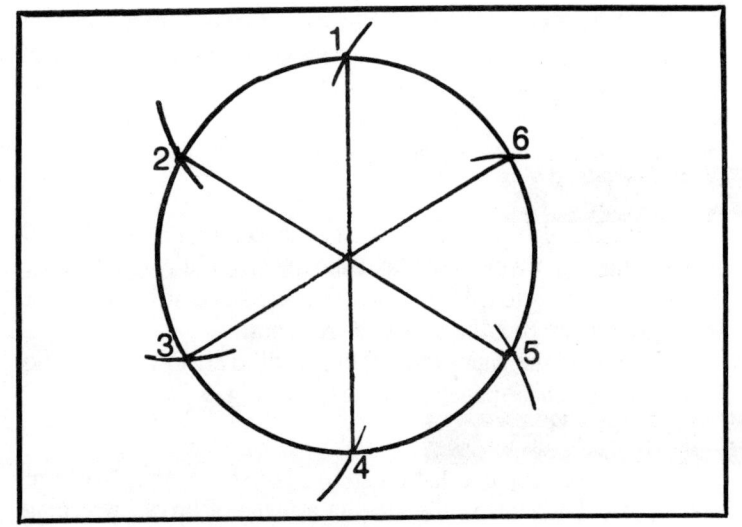

Fig. 9-1. Dividing a circle into six equal parts.

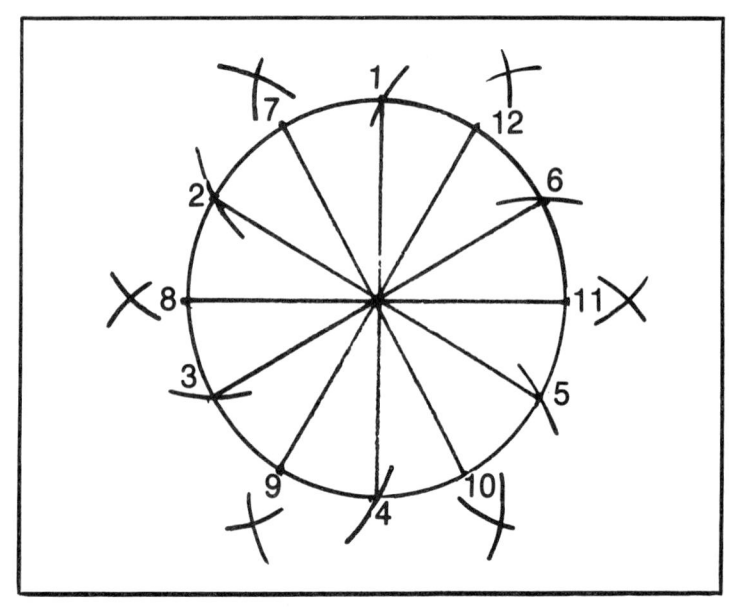

Fig. 9-2. Dividing a circle into 12 equal parts.

around the circle until you have crossed arcs outside the circle between 3 and 4, 4 and 5, and 5 and 6, making them as you go up to 11. You will have six dots outside the circle. Draw a line from each dot to the center, and you will have your circle divided into 12 equal parts (Fig. 9-2).

To make it easy to copy the design, put your compass point in the center of your circle and make faint circles at the outside and inside of each design. This will give you the size each portion should be. It is a little easier to copy this type of design this way than it is to copy it if it is squared.

CURLING PAPER

Use this process when you want curls for hair, or just a curved paper at the top of a petal or leaf. Hold the paper in your left hand. With the scissors closed and held in the right hand, draw the paper through between your thumb and the scissors.

If you hold the paper too tightly, it will tear. Practice a little before doing it on the paper you wish to use (Fig. 9-3).

ENLARGING A PATTERN

If the measurement that the design is to be is on the pattern, make the outside shape the size on a piece of brown wrapping paper. Each block of the design will be made larger proportionally

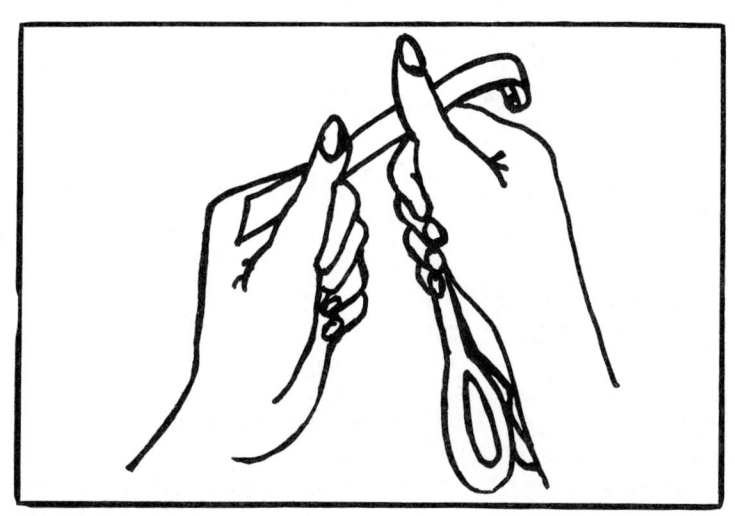

Fig. 9-3. Curling paper.

than the illustration. See Fig. 9-4. If the design is marked 7" × 8" and there are seven blocks across and eight blocks down on the design, then each block respresents 1".

On some illustrations each block may represent more than an inch or less than an inch, depending on how much it is to be enlarged. See Figs. 9-5 and 9-6.

In Fig. 9-5 there are five blocks across and six down. It is to be enlarged to 20" across by 30" down. This means that each block represents 4", with 2" left over at the bottom, or five blocks across and 7½ blocks down.

If no measurement is given, you can make the design whatever size you wish as long as you keep the same proportions.

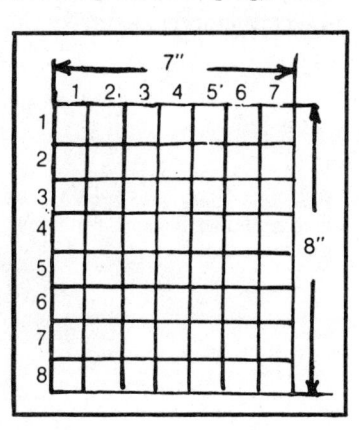

Fig. 9-4. 7"=8" design pattern.

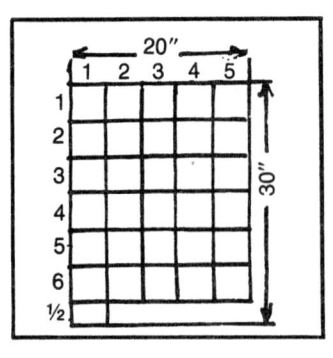

Fig. 9-5. Each block represents 4".

See Fig. 9-7. If there are six blocks across, each block can represent 1", ½", 2", 3" or whatever size you want. Each block down must then represent the same size.

After enlarging the outline, break it up into the number of blocks in the illustration and number each block. The top block across and down will be 1. Copy the design by taking up the same space in each block that is taken in the small ones, line going in the same direction and meeting the next block at the same place. Copy the design block by block.

TIPS ON PAINTING

Different types of material require different types of paint. Some paints are flat but can be made to shine by giving them a coat of acrylic spray. Some will not take this spray, so before you paint anything check the material you are using and choose your paints accordingly.

Paper and cardboard will take water colors, poster paints, crayon, chalks and liquitex, but not any oil based paint. All of these will accept an acrylic spray for shine.

Fig. 9-6. There are three blocks across and six blocks down in this pattern.

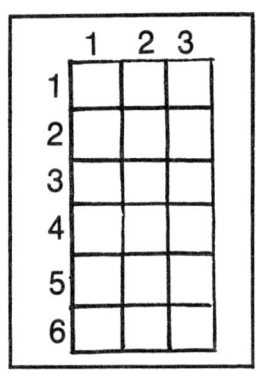

Wood will take poster paints, oil paints, house paint and enamels. Don't use acrylic spray over enamels, but the paints will accept it. Dark wood usually needs at least one coat of a flat white to make your other colors show up.

Metal and waxed surfaces will take oil paints and spray and enamel paints, but a water based color will bead up on you. If you must use a water based paint on these surfaces, add a drop or two of detergent to your paint. Be advised, though, that it will not be a permanent color.

Plastics such as the kind used on oleo lids and acetates will repel most paints. Enamels will peel off, but they can be colored very successfully with permanent ink marking pens. For gloss, use a spray of acrylic or nail polish.

Fabrics may be colored with crayon, wax, poster paints, liquitex, oils and fabric paints. If you are working on a dark fabric, it is advisable to color the whole design with at least one coat of white first.

Velour paper is like the fabric and should be treated the same way.

Glass can be painted with oil colors, but it is difficult to get smooth coverage. Of course, the glass colored becomes translucent rather than transparent. If you want a clear and smooth surface, it is best to use glass paints.

Leather can also be colored with oil paints. You will obtain the best results if you use leather dyes or stains.

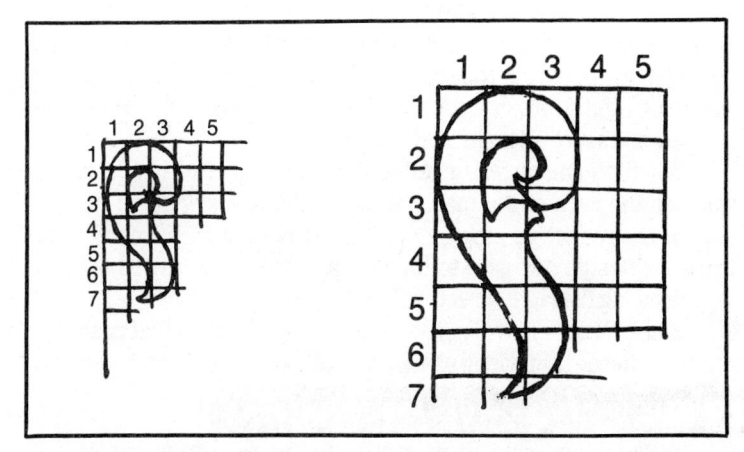

Fig. 9-7. Make the design whatever size you wish as long as you keep the same proportions.

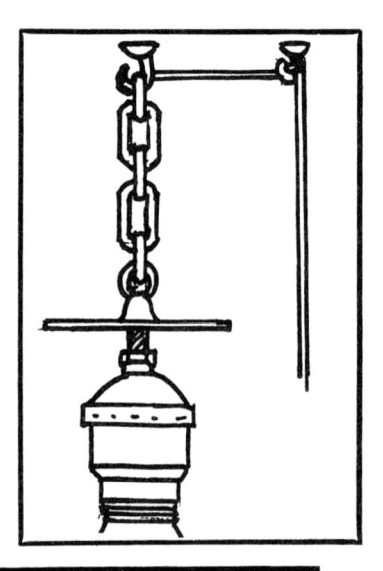

Fig. 9-8. Assembly for a swag light.

SOME TIPS ON TRACING

Many times it is necessary to use carbon paper for tracing. Some materials will take nothing else. However, there are other materials you can use on paper, cardboard, dark materials, etc.

You may have to trace on dark paper or material. If you cover the back side of the design with a good coating of white or yellow chalk, it will show up. It, however, will smear as you work, so it is a good idea after tracing to go over those chalk lines with a white or yellow crayon.

When tracing onto other paper or cardboard, you can also use carbon. Go over the back side of the design with a soft pencil. To keep it from smearing too much, take a small piece of tissue paper and very lightly brush over the lead. It will take off the excess carbon and assure all lines are covered.

When tracing on foil or reflective tape, it is often necessary to trace on the back of the material as it will not show up on the foil side or the reflective tape side. If this is necessary, remember to trace the design opposite to the design. When it is turned over, it will be facing the right direction.

Some materials will reject all of these things. In that case you can trace the design with a sharp pointed tool.

POINTERS ON PASTES, GLUES AND CEMENTS

As a general rule, it is best to follow the directions on the package containing your adherent. However, there are a few exceptions such as when you are adhering two different types of material together.

There are special types for paper, cardboard, foam plastic, fabric, leather and metal. When adhering fabric or paper to metal, however, it's a good idea to use a jewelry cement or an epoxy.

Leather will hold together with rubber cement. If you are adding another material to the leather, use an epoxy glue to be safe.

If fabrics are to withstand washing, never use a water soluble glue. Make sure the article is dry cleaned if you do, or use a glue made especially for washable fabrics.

Metal will hold to metal with a good jeweler's cement. If the metal will be subject to a great deal of stress, it is better to solder.

Contact paper, self adherent materials and tapes will adhere to soft plastic, metal, paper, cardboard, wood and metal. They will not adhere to fabrics for very long. You can use fabric glue.

When applying something like glitter to fabric, it is usually necessary to use at least two coats of the glue. The fabric or velour papers are very porous.

ASSEMBLING A SWAY LIGHT

Figure 9-8 explains the process. You will find the light easier to assemble if you attach the electrical parts before you assemble the lampshade or sides and bottom.

Push the wire through the hole in the top of your lamp and attach it to the socket. Screw into the top of the socket the hexagon-shaped bolt that holds a hexagon nut. Attach this through the hole in the top of your bottle. Attach to the top of that the round screw top that has a ring in it. The wire will go through all these things.

Open a link of your chain and connect it to the round ring. From there to the place from which you will hang your lamp, lace the cord in and out of the links. When you have reached the height you desire, hang the cup hanger and link your last link over it.

Stretch your wire across to another hanger that will be above your floor socket. Let it hang down until it reaches the plug.

Index

A
A Small Screen	50
African Necklace	220
Angel Wall Decoration	132
Ant House	214
Antique China Piece Plant Holder	241
Apple Dolls	207
Arrow Head Necklace	99
Assembling a Swag Light	293
Autograph Dachshund	241
Aztec Sun God Pendant	89

B
Baby Shower Centerpiece and Favors	184
Barbecue Apron	115
Barn Lumber Bookcase	82
Barn Lumber Cookie Cutter Holder	83
Bean Board Backdrop	275
Bed Lamp 18	
Bell Pull for Christmas	133
Belt Holder	187
Bike Backpack	242
Bill Collector	238
Birch Bark Napkin Holder	67
Bird Cage Cover	270
Bird Nest Garden	233
Book Cover	224
Bottle Lady	246
Bookmarker	218
Bookplate	217
Bookworm Bookends	110
Braided Mats	52
Branches and Berries Picture	36
Brass Wire Pin	85
Brick Doorstop	47
Bridal Shower Centerpiece and Place Mats	184
Brook Clay Figures	253
Broom Corn Swag	159
Broomstick Horse	274
Broomstick Skirt	238
Burr Porcupine	190
Button Art	250
Butterfly Bobby Pin	109
Butterfly Case	282
Butterfly Mobile	56
Butterfly Net	282
Butterfly Stretcher	283

C
Cake Pan Pictures	41
Candlestick Holders	136
Car Bag	242
Cardboard Dolls	128
Carry-All Bag	237
Carving Clay	285
Cat Collar	267
Catnip Bag	269
Cheese Box Ottoman	56
Cheese Cutting Board	113
Chessmen From Spools	196
Chickadee Feeder	263
Choirboys for Christmas	160
Christmas Bells From Paper Cups	142
Christmas Centerpiece	158
Christmas Door Decoration	131
Christmas Nut Cup	164
Christmas Sleigh	160
Christmas Tree Ornament	136
Christmas Window Decoration	136
Clam Shell Garden	236
Clay Flowers	258
Clay Mouse Pin	95
Clay Reciepe	284
Clay Trivet	56
Clothespin Clip	196
Clove Apple	101
Clover Leaf Jewelry	85
Cocktail Apron	114
Coconut Shell Lamp	15
Coffee Can Banks	247
Collection of Seashells	238
Comb Case	103
Conch Shell	77
Cork Coasters	55
Corn Husk Dolls	206
Corsage Favors	181
Corsage Holder	117
Covered Hangers	112
Cup and Saucer Man	246
Curling Paper	288
Curtain Pulls	29
Curtain Room Divider	60
Cutout Signs	233
Cutting Board	76

D
Decorated Dog Dish	267
Della Robbia Wreath	140

Depression Plant or Crystal Garden	209
Desk Blotter	108
Driftwood Planter	33
Dog Blanket	269
Dog Collar	266
Dog or Cat Bed	272
Doghouse	273
Dollhouse	104
Door Bells	81
Door Handle Cover	143

E
Easel Picture	121
Easter Candy Cup	177
Easter Centerpiece	176
Easy Candlemaking	255
Easy Christmas Cards	230
Eggs Heads	173
Egg Shell Vase	202
Egg Stand	153
Egg Tree	153
Embossed Silver Box	118
Enlarging a Pattern	288
Etched Glass	68

F
Fabric Crayon Craft	245
Fancy Balloon	181
Fancy Easter Eggs	158
Fancy Jelly Covers	128
Feather Stationary	101
Felt Change Purse	240
Felt Pencil Case	245
Finger Paint Recipe	285
Floor Plant Stand	27
Flower Arranging Vase	28
Flower Basket	109
Flower Girl Picture	36
Flowerpot Base	240
Foam Ball Christmas Decoration	136
Foam Ball Pin Cushion	109

G
Gem Tree	139
Glasses Case	103
Glitter Wall Decoration	34
Gourd Ashtray	54
Gourd Birdhouse	264
Gourd Rattle	247
Gourds On a Braid	65
Grape Pin	95

H
Hair Clip for a Page Clip	226
Hair Spray Cover-Up	52
Halloween Favor	178
Halloween Mobile	144
Halloween Nut Cup	179
Halloween Skeleton	151
Hand Print	120
Handle Holder	66
Hanging Basket Lettuce Crisper	204
Hanging Flowerpot Holder	28
Hanging Plant Holder	11
Hanging Planter From a Milk Carton	24
Heart Pin	90
Horse Tail	278
How To Divide Cricles Into Six and 12 Equal Parts	286

I
Ice Candles	195
Ice Hockey Puck	274
Indian Headband	257

J
Japanese Garden	210
Jar Pictures	204
Jewelry Box for Dad	92
Jewelry From Pull-Off Caps of Metal Cans	86

K
Key Hanger	79
Key Holders	233
Kissing Ring	138
Kitchen Table	83
Kitchen Witch	154

L
Lambkin	192
Lamp Base	20
Large Clay Planter	22
Lawn or Plant Birds	27
Leather and Foil Barrette	102
Leather Belt	219
Leather Pendant	94
Leather Picture	38

Lens Pendant	97
Leopard Doorstop	46
Letter Opener	119
Link Belt	222

M
Macaroni Beads	130
Marble Bag	244
Marble Top Table	84
Martian Paperweights	204
Mason Jar Gardens	114
Memory Box	215
Merry-Go-Round Mobile	129
Milk Carton Vase	23
Milkweed Pod Angel	139
Milkweed Pod Picture	251
Mirror Decoration	49
Mister Potato Head	191
Moccasin Decorating	240
Modern Clay Pendant	99
Mole Toy	241
Monk Doorstop	48
Mouse Repellent for a Bird Cage	273
Muffin Tin Caddy	245
Mushroom for Decorating Plants	33

N
Nail Keg Stools and Lamp Holders	84
Name Pins	205
Nature Creations On Notepaper	227
Needle Holder	239

O
Old Dough Box	77
Old Fashioned Oil Lamp	188
Old Snowflake Glass	100
Outside Hanging Lamp	12
Owl Felt Pin	99

P
Paper Bag Halloween Masks	201
Paper Bag Puppets	199
Paper Napkin Holder	67
Paper Plate Decor	262
Paper Posy	171
Patch Fun	218
Peach Stone Ducks	188
Pencil Holder	234
Pennsylvania Dutch Hex Signs	44
Photo Album Cover	234
Picture Frames	83
Pinata	254
Pine Cone Christmas Tree	141
Pine Cone Toys	280
Pine Cone Turkey	171
Pine Needle Art—Pine Needle Shapes	128
Place Cards	168
Planter Bookends	25
Plastic Snowman	163
Plastic Tomato Basket Decoration for a Door	157
Play Blocks	214
Pointers On Pastes, Glues and Cements	292
Popsicle Trellis for a Plant	81
Pot Holders	65
Potato Prints	191
Prune and Marshmallow Favor	180
Pumpkin Fun	153

Q
Quart Jar and Wine Bottle Lamps	16

R
Rag Book	240
Rattan Basket	70
Recipe for Salt Dough Christmas Tree Decorations	284
Re-doing An Old Bathroom Sink	77
Recipe for Dried Flower Mix	285
Recipe for Soft Clay for Modeling	285
Refrigerator Stickups	64
Reminder Board	254
Rhythm Sticks	279
Robot Marionette	197
Rock Collection	232
Rope Holder	261
Rubber Cord Bracelet	90

S
Salad Bowl Gardening	127
Salt and Pepper Shakers	62
Sand Scenes	30
Sand Shovel	277
Scarecrow	183
Scoring Paper or Cardboard	286
Scratch Post for a Cat	271

Scrubbers	82
Scuffs	220
Seashell Picture	43
Seed Fun	261
Seed Picture	261
Sewing Cards	232
Shadow Box	77
Shelf Covering	82
Shell Bird	261
Shell Decor	238
Silhouette Picture	41
Sit-Upon	81
Slate Pin	96
Small Pie Pan Pictures	40
Smoke Printing	223
Smoking Stand	59
Snow Jar	114
Sock Dolls	239
Soda Carrier Tote Box	255
Some Tips On Tracing	287
Spatter Print Bridge Tally Card	203
Spice Rope	125
Sponge Garden	33
Spool Toys	274
Stained Glass Swag Lamp	14
Standing Angel	161
Star Earrings	94
Stenciled Place Mats	51
Stenciled Scarf	116
Step Ladder Fun	84
Stilts	276
Stone Bug Paperweight	253
Straw Wreaths	127
String Pot	68
Suede Cloth Vest	236
Suet Baskets and Bird Cakes	265
Sugar Plum Tree	163
Swag Light	17
Swedish Kissing Ball	141
Sweet Potato Garden	210
Swirl Jar	249

T
Table Savers for Flower Pots	12
Teenagers' Birthday Party Center piece and Favors	185
Terrariums	126
Thanksgiving Centerpiece	182
Tiepin	100
Tin Can Bird Feeder	263
Tin Can Bracelet	89
Tin Can Lanterns	19
Tin Can or Tin Can Lid Coasters	72
Tiny Cushion Scents	103
Tips On Painting	290
Tiptoe Trellis	279
Tray Fun	66
Treasure Box	194
Tree House	279
Triple Candle Holder	143

U
Underwater Scene Candle Cover	211

V
Valentine Candy Cup	172
Valentine Cards	227
Valentine Centerpiece	170

W
Wall Decoration of Chinese Characters	36
Walnut Shell Bouquet	180
Walnut Shell Sailboat	190
Walnut Shell Turtle	239
Wastebasket	105
Water Garden	129
Watering Can Fun	117
Wastepaper Basket Magic	63
Winter Time Centerpiece	158
Wire and Bead Ring	88
Wooden Bead Folks and Wildlife	258
Wooden Bird or Flower Pin	86
Wooden Hangers	121
Wooden Rings Picture	43
Wooden Spoon Decor	76
Wooden Tray	62
Wooden Wren House	265
Wrapping Presents	286

Y
Yard Sign	74
Yarn Dollies	208
Yarn Holder	106
Youngsters' Birthday Party Centerpiece and Favors	185

Edited by Robert E. Ostrander